Watches

A Collector's Guide

Watches

A Collector's Guide

Frankie Leibe

Special Consultant:
Johnny Wachsmann

MILLER'S WATCHES: A COLLECTOR'S GUIDE
by Frankie Leibe
Special consultant: Johnny Wachsmann

First published in Great Britain in 1999 by Miller's, a division of
Mitchell Beazley, imprints of Octopus Publishing Group Ltd.,
Michelin House, 81 Fulham Road, London SW3 6RB

Miller's is a registered trademark of Octopus Publishing Group Ltd.

Copyright © Octopus Publishing Group 1999 Ltd.

The publishers will be grateful for any information that will assist them in
keeping future editions up to date. Although all reasonable care has been
taken in the preparation of this book, neither the publishers nor the compilers
can accept any liability for any consequence arising from the use thereof,
or the information contained therein.

ISBN 1 84000 063 5

A CIP catalogue record for this book is available from the British Library

Set in Bembo, Frutiger and Shannon
Colour reproduction by Vimnice Printing Press Co. Ltd., Hong Kong
Produced by Toppan Printing Co., (HK) Ltd.
Printed and bound in China

contents

Introduction

The earliest watches, made at the beginning of the 16thC, were spherical or drum-shaped, with single hour hands and unreliable mechanical movements. As the 21stC approaches, collectors can see how these cumbersome early portable timepieces – luxury items of their time – have evolved to become the wafer thin, light, quartz wristwatches, accurate to within fractions of a second, that are an essential part of the frenetic modern lifestyle. What has remained untouched by nearly 500 years of evolution, however, is the unique combination of artistic imagination and technical precision that makes watches such a fascinating collecting area.

The sheer number and variety of watches available are so great that all this book sets out to do is give the novice collector a very brief overview of how watches developed and the different types available, and lots of practical advice on what to look out for when buying. Detailed and in-depth accounts of the history and technical development of the watch are covered in the books listed in **What to read** (see p.62), and any would-be collector would do well to spend at least six months just reading round the subject, visiting collectors' groups, dealers, specialist auctions, antique shops, museums, markets (remember to take a torch to make sure you can really see what you're buying), and so on (see **Where to buy** p.62) just in order to become familiar with the field.

By the time you have an idea of what is available in your price range you may already have decided which area – a particular era perhaps, or style – you are interested in collecting. In general, the earlier the watch, the rarer and more expensive it will prove. But the beauty of collecting watches is choice: although a good 17thC pocket watch is outside the budget of all but the most affluent of collectors, a 17thC movement or watch cock may well be a possibility. Similarly, if you are primarily interested in the movements, buy one that is uncased or housed in an inexpensive or damaged case. Whatever you choose, it pays to buy the very best that you can afford – the finest examples in any area will hold their values and enable you to trade up as your knowledge widens and your tastes change.

With this in mind, try to build up a relationship with a reliable dealer who can advise you and guide you through what can be an expensive minefield. He or she will be able to advise on restoration. A good restorer, if you can find one, should be prepared to give you a quotation and provide a clear explanation of what work is to be carried out. Restoration is rarely inexpensive, however, so do bear in mind that a watch at a "bargain" price may ultimately cost you far more after restoration than another initially more expensive example that is in much better condition. A good dealer may also be prepared to help you trade up (check what percentage of purchase price is offered), will provide an invoice and should be prepared to do repairs at cost price within three months of purchase.

Watches are small, and finding space for a collection is rarely a problem, but they do need to be kept in a dry (but not overheated), dustfree environment, and working watches should be run at least three or four times a year. Security can be a problem, as watches are eminently suited to swift and unobtrusive removal (never buy one that is offered in remotely suspicious circumstances); many insurance companies do offer specialist collectors' insurance but may insist upon certain security arrangements.

If you haven't already decided on a particular area, the broad guidelines that follow may be of some help. Although relatively common during the 1980s, good early 18thC watches are becoming rare and expensive; similarly, good, clean, late 19thC Swiss and English precision watches are also increasingly hard to find. Military, form, and erotic watches, and automatons are always popular, and American watches are almost a field on their own. In general, the more modern a watch, the better its condition must be if it is to be of any value; mass-produced plastic watches need to be in original packaging and in mint condition.

It is also worth addressing the question of accuracy in old movements, which is often a matter of compromise. Verges, for example, may have a perfectly acceptable gain or loss of thirty minutes a day; cylinders may vary by ten minutes a day. Worn duplexes, rack levers, and chronometers may gain or lose between ten and thirty minutes a day; if in good condition, that figure will be reduced to between two and five minutes. An early 19thC lever may gain or lose two to three minutes a day, whereas for a lever watch made towards the end of the century that figure would be 30 to 90 seconds.

Finally, and to reiterate, watches that have been well-maintained are more expensive initially. But while a watch in good condition that costs £100 will hold its value and quite possibly appreciate, two £50 watches bought in poor condition will probably cost at least twice their price to restore properly and won't reach the value of an unrestored original or appreciate to the same extent. This also applies if you buy movements, dials, or other components and accessories. Whatever area you choose to collect, and however modest your budget might be, invest in quality, and time will reward you.

Prices and dimensions

Condition is of paramount importance when deciding the value of a watch. The price ranges given in this book reflect "fair" to "excellent" condition. Prices for antiques also vary according to geographical location and market trends, so the price ranges given throughout this book should be seen as guides to value only.

Abbreviations used for dimensions are as follows: **l.** length; **w.** width.

Dimensions are given in both centimetres and inches. Watches are not shown to scale.

The parts of a watch

All the many different components that go to make up a watch play a part in its collectability, so it is important to examine them carefully and systematically before buying. There is no substitute for experience and guidance from a reliable dealer, but the following checklist will be a useful aide-mémoire when you are dazzled by the huge number and variety of watches available.

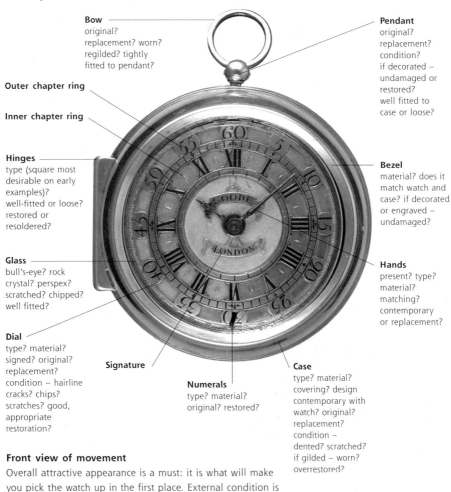

Bow
original?
replacement? worn?
regilded? tightly
fitted to pendant?

Pendant
original?
replacement?
condition?
if decorated –
undamaged or
restored?
well fitted to
case or loose?

Outer chapter ring

Inner chapter ring

Hinges
type (square most
desirable on early
examples)?
well-fitted or loose?
restored or
resoldered?

Bezel
material? does it
match watch and
case? if decorated
or engraved –
undamaged?

Glass
bull's-eye? rock
crystal? perspex?
scratched? chipped?
well fitted?

Hands
present? type?
material?
matching?
contemporary
or replacement?

Dial
type? material?
signed? original?
replacement?
condition – hairline
cracks? chips?
scratches? good,
appropriate
restoration?

Signature

Numerals
type? material?
original? restored?

Case
type? material?
covering? design
contemporary with
watch? original?
replacement?
condition –
dented? scratched?
if gilded – worn?
overrestored?

Front view of movement
Overall attractive appearance is a must: it is what will make you pick the watch up in the first place. External condition is also a good guide to internal condition.

Back and side view of movement

Open the case – case springs and hinges should work smoothly – and take out the movement. If it drops out or sticks, it may not be the original. The bezel and movement hinges should also work smoothly, with the movement swinging out easily and evenly.

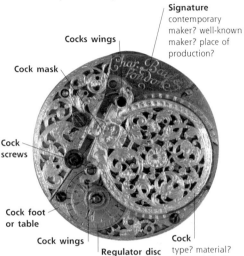

Cock mask

Cocks wings

Signature
contemporary maker? well-known maker? place of production?

Cock screws

Cock foot or table

Cock wings

Regulator disc

Cock
type? material? decorated and engraved? condition – damaged or resoldered? original screws?

Pillars
type? material? number? pierced galleries above? affixes present or missing?

Fusee

Back or top plate

Dial plate
signed? clean? scratched? gilding complete?

Escapement
type? original or modified? converted to other type of escapement?

Cases TYPES: consular, form, half hunter, (full) hunter, open face, pair case. MARKS: pre-1700, maker's initial, no hallmark; after *c.*1710, maker's initials; English hallmarks (usually); sometimes numbered same as movement. MATERIALS: gilt, gold, rock crystal, silver, steel. COVERINGS: enamel, horn, shagreen, tortoiseshell.

Dials TYPES: cartouche, champlevé enamel, chronograph, digital, double dial, duodial, engine-turned, engraved, subsidiary seconds, two-tone, two- and three-piece. MATERIALS: enamel (white, eggshell, polychrome, coloured), gilt, gold, ivory, mother-of-pearl, silver, silvered, steel. MARKS: maker's and/or retailer's signature on face; well-known makers sometimes signed dial plate as well to avoid forgeries.

Hands TYPES: arrow, beetle and poker, Breguet or "moon", fleur-de-lys, half hunter, reverse dart, tulip. MATERIALS: blued steel, gilt, gold, silver.

Movements MATERIALS: brass, almost always plated; earlier examples are fire or mercury gilt. MARKS: signed on back plate with maker's name and address (often abbreviated), and numbered.

Cocks TYPES: Continental (bridge cock secured to plate by two diametrically opposed screws), English (cock with large foot screwed to plate), engraved, historical, hunting, masked, musical, pierced, winged.

Pillars TYPES: Egyptian, plain, round, square baluster, tulip. MATERIALS: brass, gilt brass, silver, brass and silver affixes. NUMBER: most watches have 3–6 pillars.

Numerals TYPES: arabic, batons, other (export watches), roman, turkish. MATERIALS: cartouche, champlevé enamel, gilt, gold, painted, silver.

Escapements & mechanical parts

A watch is classified by its movement, or, strictly speaking, its escapement. Movement is the term used to describe the mechanics beneath the dial that activate the timekeeping; the escapement is the part of the movement that connects the mainspring power and the regulator. Or, very simply, the movement is the engine of the watch while the escapement is the piston. Watchmakers experimented with hundreds of different types of escapement in the search for ever more accurate timekeeping. Detailed descriptions can be found in the works listed in **What to read** (*see* p.62); this section will outline the most common types of escapement shown in this book.

▼ Verge

The verge was used from the early 16thC up until the first half of the 19thC, when it was gradually replaced by the lever (the verge is rarely found on watches produced after 1850). It is also known as the "crown-wheel escapement" because the escape wheel, with its 11 or 13 teeth, looks like a crown. It's long life was due to the fact that it was a reliable workhorse; it was, however, rather large, not particularly accurate, and in need of constant power (provided by a vulnerable fusee chain).

▼ Cylinder

Perfected by the English maker George Graham (1675–1751) in 1726, this escapement was particularly popular in the late 18thC in France, where it was used to make slimmer watches. Impulse is provided by wedge-shaped teeth that enter an aperture in the hollow cylinder carrying the balance. Although superseded in England by the lever from c.1830, the cylinder was still seen as a competitive alternative on the continent.

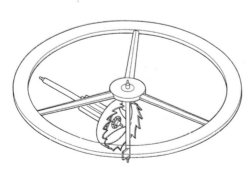

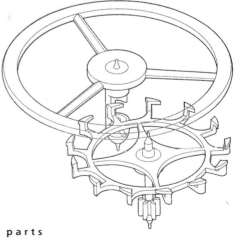

▼ Duplex

Although several watchmakers of varying nationalities are associated with the invention of the duplex, a modified and improved version was patented by the English watchmaker Thomas Tyrer in 1782, and the escapement was mainly used in England as a high-quality alternative to the verge until c.1850. The escape wheel has two sets of teeth: one long and pointed that locks, the other small and wedge-shaped that provides the impulse to a pallet mounted on the balance staff. Sometimes the pallet is jewelled. Occasionally the two sets of teeth are mounted on two separate wheels. The advantage of this escapement is that the balance can swing freely, with little friction.

▼ Chronometer

In France and Switzerland a chronometer is any watch with an official rating certificate; in Britain it is a watch that has a detent escapement. John Arnold (1736–99) and Thomas Earnshaw (1749–1829) – two English watchmakers – were at the heart of its development. Arnold worked first on a version with a pivoted detent and then on one with a spring detent. In Earnshaw's version, developed in the mid-1780s, the detent is sprung about one end and has a jewel standing proud of the surface that holds the escape wheel and locks the train. This escapement made possible accurate and reliable timekeepers that were to play an important part in ensuring British horological and naval supremacy (its development was due to the fact that a prize of £20,000, a huge sum in the 18thC, was offered by the Board of Longitude).

FACT FILE

• 1745–1840: a great variety of escapements was made, so collectors have plenty of choice.
• After 1840: choice is more limited after the classic English lever became standard in stock English watches, and makers concentrated on high-grade precision timepieces.
• It is difficult to inspect beneath the dial; collectors will have to trust the vendor that the dial and motion work are compatible with the watch, and that no major changes have been made.
• Movements should be complete. Check that all of the components are similar in colour to ensure that no part has been replaced, and check for unexplained holes in the plates.
• Movements should be clean with few, if any, scratches (implying bad repair work), especially around the pins of the top plate.
• Give one-and-a-half turns of the winding mechanism to check that the movement springs into action.

▼ Rack lever escapement

Although the idea was conceived by a Frenchman in 1722, it was a watchmaker from England, Peter Litherland (1756–1800), who developed the rack lever escapement into a practical form and patented it in 1791 and 1792. The most common form features a right-angled layout in which the lever ends in a rack, the teeth of which mesh with a pinion on the balance staff. The rack lever was a simpler escapement than the cylinder, duplex, or chronometer, and it provided the first robust and cheap alternative to the verge. It was much used in Liverpool, where watchmakers made it on a semi-mass-production basis, and from where rack lever watches were often exported to the USA.

▲ English lever

The distinctive feature of this type of escapement is that only the tips of the 15 pointed teeth on the escape wheel are in contact with the pallet, which means that all the lift is on the pallets. The escapement used the fusee with maintaining power, which meant that the watch could be wound without losing time or stopping. Robust and accurate, it was invented c.1759 by Thomas Mudge (1715–94), who, thinking it too difficult for most makers, decided not develop it. Examples dating from before 1810 are very rare, but the escapement was improved by English makers, and English lever watches were produced in quantity between 1820 and 1920.

▼ Swiss lever

An evolution of the English lever, the Swiss lever was perfected by Swiss makers in the mid-19thC; its advantage was that there was less wear to the escape wheel, as the lift was distributed to the pallets. Unlike the tips of the English lever's teeth, those here are flattened. The Swiss is mainly found as a straight-line lever in which the wheel, lever and balance staff are all arranged on a straight line. With other improvements to the balance and the spring, the Swiss lever proved very accurate without the expense of a fusee and chain. It soon almost entirely replaced all other types of escapement, and is still used in mechanized wristwatches.

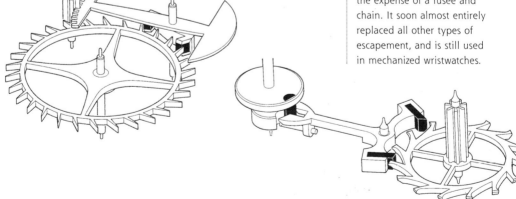

▼ Fusee and gut

The fusee had been used in clocks since the mid-15thC to equalize the power of the mainspring (which means that the power transferred to the balance is the same whether the watch is fully wound or nearly wound down). It was adapted from its original purpose for use in watches. Cone shaped, the fusee has spiral grooves, for gut at first and then for chain (invented c.1635, and virtually standard from 1680), which was less susceptible to perishing and variations in temperature. English makers continued to use fusee-driven movements until the early 20thC, long after Continental and American makers had abandoned them in favour of the going barrel.

▼ Going barrel

With the replacement of the verge by the cylinder and lever escapements, which did not require a constant torque, it became feasible to take the impulse direct from a "going barrel" – a barrel that had an integral wheel. Continental makers used the going barrel from the late 19thC, while American makers used it as early as 1850. English makers did not wholeheartedly adopt it until the end of the 19thC. The advantages of the going barrel were that it was simple, reduced the size of the movement, and obviated the need for a fragile fusee chain.

• Fusee and chain: wind the watch fully to check that the length of chain is sufficient for the fusee; check that the fusee stop mechanism is working – if it is not, overwinding will break the chain.

• Check that the watch works when held in different positions: dial up and down; pendant up and down; pendant right and left. If it stops with the dial face down, it may have a broken jewel or balance staff; if it stops in any of the pendant positions, the jewel may be cracked or the staff bent.

• Check that the hands line up properly by setting the watch at 6, 12, 9 and 3 o'clock.

• Repeaters: only rotate hands clockwise! Activate at the following times to ensure full range: quarter repeaters at 12.50, and minute repeaters at 12.59 and 1.01.

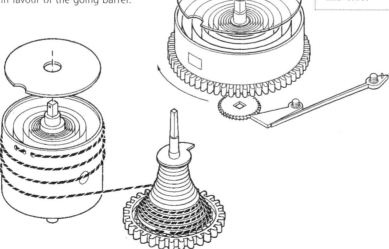

1650–1700: French & English watches

Until the late 17thC, watches were luxury ornamental items rather than accurate timekeepers, and French makers were pre-eminent until their English counterparts made important technical advances. Thomas Tompion (1637–1713) was instrumental, c.1675, in developing the balance spring, which enabled watches to be accurate to within a few minutes. Hour and minute hands replaced the single hour hand, and arabic minute numerals appeared on the dial in addition to roman hour numerals. In 1687, Daniel Quare (1647–1724) patented a repeating mechanism that sounded the hours and quarter hours. After 1685, when Huguenot craftsmen fled to London, there was much cross-fertilization of styles; it remained, however, that French watches, unlike those made in England and Germany, did not have pair cases and were wound through the dial, rather than the back.

◀ Silver case

Blois, in France, was home to several leading watchmakers, among them Theodore Girard (1596–1680). Several factors make this example collectable. First, it is in extremely good condition: the cast chased and engraved silver case has 12 panels and shows no signs of wear, which bodes well for the internal workings. The finely engraved silver dial has the single hand and roman numerals typical of the time. As with many early watches, some parts have been replaced: in this case a later silver bow and pendant have been added. Provided that the style is appropriate, such later additions are quite acceptable on a watch of this period.

French pre-balance spring verge, c.1640, signed "Theodore Girard Blois", £12,500–16,000

▶ Rock crystal case

The fashion for rock crystal jewellery was reflected in the vogue for rock crystal watch cases between c.1600 and 1675. While hardwearing, rock crystal is vulnerable to knocks, and restoration can be difficult. The slightly bent original pendant on this example has been left, since repair would risk breaking the case. Scratches suggest a case may be glass, not rock crystal, and therefore less collectable. Rock crystal was usually accompanied by a gold champlevé dial, as seen here. The maker, Solomon Bouquet (active 1680–1700), worked in London but may well have been French.

English verge, c.1680, signed "S Bouquet London", £6,000–8,000

▼ Oignon alarm

The alarm on this watch was designed to be used at night, when the timepiece would have been stood up, with the front bezel open, so that the alarm could be clearly heard through the elegant piercing and engraving on the inside of the watch. The white enamel cartouche numerals, which were almost exclusively found on French watches, are sought-after features. Most will have been restored, but good restoration, in which the colour of the enamel and the painted numerals match the originals, is acceptable. Another French feature is the continental-style table cock with a partial cutout and a mock pendulum as part of the balance wheel. Oignon (onion) derives from the bulbous shape and the outer skin of silver or brass applied to the case, which here has a further decorative layer of shagreen over the gilt metal.

French verge with alarm, c.1690, signed "Pia à Paris", **£2,000–6,000**

English verge, c.1695, signed "Fromanteel & Clarke", **£2,200–3,500**

▲ Silver pair case

The London-based partnership of Fromanteel & Clarke (active c.1695–1700) was known for high-quality attractive watches. This example has two hands in the beetle and poker style common on English watches from c.1690, and the silver champlevé dial (very popular at the time) has roman hour and arabic minute numerals. Pair cases were introduced in the mid-17thC. The outer case protected the decorative inner case, but by c.1690 the outer cases were more common and more elaborately decorated – watches would sometimes have a third case in order to protect the outer case.

- On examples of pair-cased watches, outside and inside cases should match. The watch should sit well in its case and fit properly, while the pendant should fit snugly in its aperture.
- Silver cases were not hallmarked at this time and usually bear only the casemaker's initials.
- Movements are usually signed.
- Square hinges were used until 1700; the best have seven joints.
- Some wear on more vulnerable parts – hinges, thumbpiece, and pendant – is acceptable.

English verge with alarm, c.1695, signed "Quare London", **£4,000–10,000**

▲ Silver alarm

Watches by Quare are sought after, and this example has the added appeal of an alarm. The style of the silver repoussé outer case suggests that it was made ten to fifteen years later than the watch. This apparent discrepancy is quite common, as owners often commissioned new cases as styles changed.

1700–60: decorative watches

Technical advances included the use of jewels as bearings to reduce friction and the development of the horizontal cylinder escapement (*c.*1700) by either Thomas Tompion or his apprentice George Graham (1673/4–1751). England and France remained the major centres of production, and, with the comparative lull in technical developments, watchmakers concentrated on decoration. Repoussé work developed from radial fluting to a golden age (1725–50) of elaborate allegorical and mythical scenes. White enamel – easier to read than champlevé – replaced metal on dials and was standard by 1750. Further decoration took the form of hand-painted scenes of rural pursuits, famous battles, commemorative subjects, and portraits.

▶ **Silver pair case**
This watch combines exceptionally good condition with several unusual features. David Lestourgeon was born in Rouen and came to London in 1680, where he established a reputation as "a fine maker". His French background is shown in the unusual large pierced and engraved continental bridge cock, which has a parcel-gilt silver cartouche in the centre bearing a repoussé portrait of Queen Anne. Another unusual feature is that the watch is regulated by a gilt and blued steel disc fitted below the numeral XII on the fine silver champlevé dial. These features, combined with the excellent condition of the watch, make it most attractive.

English verge, *c.*1700, signed "David Lestourgeon London 1828", **£3,500–5,000**

▼ **Silver clockwatch**
Clockwatches, unless silenced using a slide fitted below the dial, struck automatically on the hour, as did the bracket clocks that remained the main focus for German makers at this time. Although Bushmann of Augsburg was one of the better-known makers, the silver champlevé dial is inferior to coeval English examples, as is the pierced and engraved silver case. The real attraction of this watch is that it is still in working order, although close inspection reveals that the foot of the cock has been extended, which will detract from its value.

German clockwatch, *c.*1700, signed "Bushmann Augsburg", **£4,000–6,000**

Dials

• British polychrome dials are most desirable. The condition of the decoration must be excellent, as restoration of painted decoration will lower value.

• Enamel dials are vulnerable and often damaged. While hairline cracks are acceptable, more extensive damage or missing pieces are not.

• Good restoration is important; colouring and hand-painting of numerals must be virtually undetectable.

• Battle scenes, commemorative subjects, and rural pursuits are all popular themes found on polychrome dials. Masonic dials are rare and highly collectable but often faked; portraits are rare and collectable.

• The rarer the subject, the more likely it is to be faked, but the higher the value if genuine.

▼ **Gold pair case**

The 22-carat gold used in watchmaking was a soft and vulnerable material, and it is rare to find a watch of this period with its original gold dial. In this case the dial and hands are not only original but also in exceptionally good condition. The outer case, on the other hand, which has a seven-joint square hinge, is a replacement, as are the bow and pendant, but as both were purpose-made close to the original date and fit well they will not detract from the piece's value. The movement is of the same high quality, with a fine pierced and engraved wing cock. The maker of this watch, Simon Des Charmes, was of French birth but worked in London.

▼ **Plain gold pair case**

Early 18thC plain gold pair cases are rare. They were normally found with matching gold champlevé dials, but on this example the original dial has been replaced by what would have been considered a more "modern" white enamel dial. Gold cases were usually 22 carat. Their softness makes them vulnerable to dents, but with plain cases this is easy to put right; heavily engraved or initialled cases make repair more difficult. The smaller, slightly more squat shape is matched by the short pendant that is typical of this period. Windmills (1671–1723), a London-based firm, is best known for its late 17thC and early 18thC watches.

English verge, hallmarked 1711, signed "S Des Charmes London", **£3,000–4,000**

English verge, hallmarked 1728, signed "Windmills London 4838", **£3,000–5,000**

English verge, c.1705, signed "Henry Massy London 3095", **£1,600–2,200**

English fusee, c.1750, unsigned, **£3,000–6,000**

English verge with quarter repeater, c.1730, signed "John Winsmore London", **£4,000–7,000**

▲ Shagreen case

The hardwearing quality of shagreen – a form of sharkskin – made it an ideal covering for watch cases, and it was often combined with *piqué* (pinwork). Complete original shagreen cases are rare, and good re-covering will always be preferable to bad fill-ins or patches. This example was produced by Henry Massy (active 1692–1745) – a famous London maker – and the superb condition of the gilt-metal consular case covered with green shagreen (shagreen with large scales, as seen here, is the most sought after) with gilt *piqué* pins, the signed dial, and the verge movement make it highly collectable.

▲ Repoussé repeater

The excellent condition and high-quality repoussé work on the gold outer case of this quarter repeater watch are its main appeal. The exceptionally fine and unmarked condition is due to both the unusually thick gauge of the gold and the presence of a third gilt metal and leather outer case that must have been used most of the time. The Classical subject matter is typical, and the fine piercing allows the sound of the repeater bell to be heard. The original dial would have been of gold champlevé or white enamel, but it has been replaced with a Victorian dial that greatly reduces the value of the watch; nevertheless, it is still worth collecting for the superb case alone.

▲ Ivory case

It is the decorative case rather than the movement that is the major attraction of this hybrid watch. The finely engraved octagonal ivory case, with a turned ivory pendant and bow, was probably made in Dieppe, France, which at this time was a centre for ivory carving. The lid of the case is decorated with a Nativity scene, the back with a representation of God appearing before Spanish soldiers. The unusual ivory dial has a single ivory hand and roman numerals; there is further carved decoration in the form of birds and angels around the chapter ring. In contrast to fine relief work on the deliberately archaicized case, the later, purpose-made oval fusee movement is of no particular merit.

▼ Polychrome dial

Rural pursuits – the angler seen here, for example – were favourite subjects for painted polychrome dials. English examples are prized for being generally superior, but the condition of the dial is of the utmost importance since any restoration of the hand-painted decoration – detectable with ultraviolet light – will reduce value. Restoration of the unpainted area is acceptable, and on this example the white chapter has been fully restored. Although the whole dial may be decorated, it is the quality rather than the quantity of decoration that will determine value. Dutch makers were also skilful decorators at this time, and many fake "English" dials and movements were produced and combined with English hallmarked cases.

English verge, c.1760, signed "Mary Cooper London 1767", £400–1,000

▲ Gilt-metal and leather pair case

Note the signature: "Mary Cooper London 1767"; women makers were unusual, and this may in fact be the name of the owner. The white enamel dial is clear and elegant, although the original blued steel beetle and poker hands have been replaced by gilt hands, which reduces the value. The outer of the gilt metal pair case is covered in black leather with gilt *piqué* work – a feature popular with most collectors.

Cases

• The golden age of repoussé cases was 1725 to 1780. Good condition is essential – some wear is acceptable, but dents are not.

• Dents can be removed from silver and gold with little difficulty, but not from gilt-metal cases without risking the loss of the original gilding.

• Tortoiseshell cases are susceptible to changes in temperature (avoid direct heat), fade when kept in direct sunlight, and crack when reheated or struck so pique work will always prove difficult to restore. Missing pieces or major cracks will detract from value.

▼ Tortoiseshell and gilt-metal pair case

This watch has three desirable features, all in excellent condition. The white enamel dial, with blued steel beetle and poker hands, is original; the outer of the gilt metal pair case has repoussé work; and a third outer case of gilt metal is covered with red tortoiseshell with gold *piqué* work. Tortoiseshell is brittle and can be cleaned but not repaired, so major flaws will detract from value.

English verge, hallmarked London 1753, signed "Jno Smith York", £700–1,100

English verge, c.1760, signed "J Millington London", £1,300–1,700

1760–1820: decorative dials

Watches from this period are more commonly found; collectors, therefore, are more demanding about condition and restoration. New escapements were developed – lever (*c.*1750), duplex (*c.*1780), and chronometer (1780s) – which, together with the verge and cylinder, were refined and improved for several decades. Movements became less bulbous, and slim, accurate, robust timekeepers became the priority. The qualities, combined with elegance, were the hallmark of Abraham-Louis Breguet (1747–1823), one of the greatest of all watchmakers, whose clients included the royal families of Europe. White enamel continued to replace metal on dials, and calendars, commemorative subjects, and customized polychrome dials became selling points. English painted dials retained their cachet, while specialized dials were produced for the Turkish and Chinese markets.

▼ White enamel dial

This English watch is a good example of the standard white enamel dial of the period. The dial has a fine hairline crack, but such minor damage is in fact preferable to full restoration. The hands are not original, but both the material (blued steel) and the style (beetle and poker) of the replacements are appropriate. The silver pair case is original, with matching hallmarks and maker's marks (a replacement matched outer case, even by the same maker, is less desirable). The bow and pendant are original, as is the verge movement, which has square baluster pillars rather than the less sought-after round pillars.

English verge, hallmarked London 1766, signed "Jno Hays London 1132", £250–700

▼ Polychrome dial

A horse-drawn carriage is quite an unusual subject for a polychrome dial, and this one also has the owner's name – John Hayward – in place of the numerals, which is an almost exclusively English feature that makes it especially rare and collectable. Restoration on this type of dial is unacceptable unless the originality of the design can be guaranteed. The hands and the gilt pair case, all of which are original features, are other attractions. Original gilding, even if it is worn on the central back of the watch and the bow and pendant, is preferable to overbright re-gilding.

English verge, c.1780, signed "Thos Garnier London 3196", £750–1,350

▼ "English" Polychrome dial

Although typically English in its subject-matter (a hunting scene), style of painting, and brightness of colour, this dial is probably a Dutch fake. The clues to this are the arcaded decoration that separates the roman and arabic numerals, and the signature – "J Harts, London" – which, together with variants such as "Tarts" and "Farts", was often used on fakes. The English case is genuine and has original hallmarks, but the movement, although well constructed, has a continental cock and is probably not of the same quality and reliability as an English counterpart.

▼ Calendar dial

The unusual and highly decorative dial is the most important feature of this gold Swiss watch. The silver pierced mask and the bezel are set with marquesites, and three white enamel dials show the hours (top left) in roman numerals, the minutes (top right), and the date (bottom) in arabic numerals. There are pierced gilt hands for the time and blued steel hand for the calendar dial.

• Dials with unusual layouts or additional indications – calendar, moonphase, extra time zones, and so on – were rare at this time.
• Dutch fake "English" polychrome dials can be very attractive, but prices should reflect their origin and lower-quality movements.
• Polychrome dials customized with, for example, rural scenes for farmers, on which the owner's initials replace the numerals, are rare and highly sought after.
• Highly decorative dials are often collected for their visual appeal alone.

Swiss verge with calendar, c.1780, unsigned, £4,000–6,000

▼ Compass watch

The English maker Benjamin Webb (active 1781–1810), was known for compass watches. Unlike some French and Swiss examples, on which the feature was mainly decorative, the compasses on Webb's rare and highly desirable watches were operational and accurate. The movement, therefore, used as few steel pieces as possible, substituting gilt brass, and the compass was placed above the barrel in order to minimize magnetic disturbance.

English verge, hallmarked London 1762, signed "J Harts London 5583", £500–800

English verge with integral compass, hallmarked London 1799, signed "Benjn Webb London 99 By the King's Patent", £3,000–5,000

1760–1820: decorative cases

As improvements in movements and accuracy made watchmaking more competitive, watch cases changed in style. Repoussé cases gradually went out of fashion, and enamel became less common and tended to become confined to panels. Swiss makers favoured engine turning – a technique that enabled them to reduce the cost of their product. Introduced in the mid–1770s, it enhanced the effect of enamel decoration and was often used as a ground beneath a layer of translucent enamel. Tortoiseshell inlaid with silver or gold *piqué* work was popular, and underpainted horn, originally intended to simulate tortoiseshell, became used in its own right. Watches were also made to complement contemporary jewellery design.

◄ Underpainted horn

The technique used on underpainted horn was similar to that used on underpainted glass miniatures, and the work was often executed by the same artists. A piece of horn, so thin as to be almost translucent, was painted in reverse (that is to say, on the side that will be innermost) and then attached to the watch; the example shown here depicts a popular rural scene. The bezel is tortoiseshell with *piqué* decoration. Horn or tortoiseshell were usually combined with gilt metal, as here, which will often have signs of wear on the inner or outer case, but worn original gilding is always preferable to re-gilding. The well-made verge escapement and the square baluster pillars are added attractions.

English verge, c.1770, signed "J Williamson London", £450–2,000

▼ Painted miniatures

The gold consular case of this French watch is a very unusual combination of four miniature portraits of, it is thought, the King of Sardinia and George I, and, inside, their wives. Such historical subjects are rare and very desirable, and the slight crack on the inner portrait of the front cover is preferable to restoration on such a portrait. The front and back lids are solid, with no glass aperture, and seem to be an early form of the hunter case. The maker, Baillon (probably Jean Baptiste, active in Paris 1751 to c.1770), was highly regarded.

French verge, c.1770, signed "Baillon à Paris", £4,000– 10,000

English verge repeater clockwatch, c.1770, signed "Crawford London 1012", **£15,000–40,000**

English verge for Turkish market, hallmarked London 1778, signed "Benjamin Barber London 7735", **£450–2,000**

- Good silver repoussé cases are more common than gold examples as they are less vulnerable.
- Fully enamelled cases may not be hallmarked.
- Enamel portraits are rare; if historical portraits are fully restored, proof of authenticity is needed.
- Restoration of enamel cases is acceptable if it has been well executed.
- Minor cracks to horn and tortoiseshell cases are acceptable; major restoration is expensive.
- Agate cases are very rare and very valuable.

▲ Agate repeater clockwatch

The high value of this English repeating clockwatch has been determined by several factors. The rare and complicated movement is fitted with two separate trains for striking the hours and the quarter hours (the latter can be disabled by a small lever). The obvious appeal, however, is the superb agate-panelled 22-carat gold gem-set outer case. Vulnerable agate cases are rarely found in such good condition, and most have cracked or missing panels (this example has one cracked panel). Engraved and pierced for the repeater mechanism, the inner case is also in good condition, and the hands and front bezel are set with paste gems. The elaborate decoration suggests that the white enamel dial may be a replacement for an original of gold champlevé.

▲ Triple-cased export watch

English watches made for the Turkish market commonly had three cases. A plain inner case housed the movement; the second case might be plain or, as in this example, chased and engraved; and the outer case would be the most decorative. This example is silver, covered with blond tortoiseshell with engraved silver bezels and silver *piqué* work. Some of the watches for the Turkish market had a fourth case, which was made locally, to protect the elaborate third case. Typically compact in size, this watch is in unusually good condition. Produced over a long period (1760 to 1880), these watches changed little in design.

▼ Gold and enamel case

Although signed "Breguet à Paris" on the dial, this cylinder watch was almost certainly only sold by the French workshop. The polychrome enamel back of the gold case has a finely painted alpine scene, and the enamel decoration continues onto the bezels and pendant. The scene has been restored, which is quite common with enamel painted cases and also quite acceptable if well executed.

French cylinder, c.1790, signed "Breguet à Paris", **£2,000–4,000**

1760–1820: form watches

Form watches first became popular in the early 17thC, when watch cases were designed in a range of shapes or forms – skulls, crucifixes, books, dogs, birds, and so on – intended to disguise their true purpose. As 18thC technical developments enabled movements to become smaller, the form watch re-emerged, and the beauty of the tiny movements was sacrificed to the inventiveness of the form. French, Austrian, and Swiss makers in particular produced a wide range of form watches, many of which imitated jewellery. Form watches, although rare and expensive, are a very popular collecting field. Attractive appearance and ingenuity of design command premium prices.

▼ **Crucifix**
This interesting form watch (the crucifix is a common and popular shape) is a copy of an early 17thC watch. The single hand, movement, and biblical motifs are in the 17thC style, but the wheel work, colour of gilding, and overall quality of the watch identify it as 18thC. It may have been intended as a piece of jewellery, as the lack of a hairspring means that its timekeeping ability was severely limited. The unusual and complex multi-hinged case is set with rock crystal panels, allowing both movement and dial to be seen easily.

Austrian verge, c.1780, signed "Etienne Bordier fecit", **£3,000–20,000**

◀ **Watch and chatelaine**
Complete, undamaged chatelaines are rare and very sought after. This English example has all five chains: one for the watch; one for the watch key; a third for the family seal; and two spare for other implements. The design and colour of all the different elements should match. On this example the oval en-grisaille enamelled plaques and gold and enamelled link chains are echoed by the gold and enamel consular case (unusual for an English watch). Chatelaines were costly when new and are still so today. Some minor damage is acceptable; far more important is that all the elements should be present and matching.

English verge, c.1780, unsigned, **£3,000–10,000**

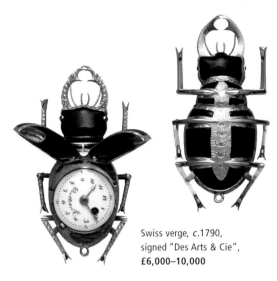

- Form watches were designed primarily for show rather than good timekeeping; appearance and ingenuity of design determine value.
- Form watches produced by Austrian, Swiss, and French makers are most sought after.
- Case mechanisms must be in good working order, as restoration or repair of spring work is extremely complicated and expensive.
- Minor damage or restoration is acceptable provided that it does not detract from the watch's appearance; hairline cracks or replaced gem stones or pastes, will not dramatically affect value, although replacement stones or pastes must match the originals.
- Chatelaines were made of various materials - gilt or silver repoussé, gold and even cut steel.
- Chatelaines are rare and sought after, and should be complete with attachments that match in design, colour, and proportion.

Swiss verge, c.1790, signed "Des Arts & Cie", **£6,000–10,000**

▲ Stag beetle

This stag beetle form watch is an early example of a design that was more common during the late 19thC. The quality is far superior to that of its later counterparts, however, and it has several ingenious features. The white enamel dial can be seen by pressing the rear legs together to open the wings. The front pincers open when the front legs are squeezed together, allowing the watch to be hung on a chain. The inventive design is matched by a fine gold and enamel case, with split pearls set in the legs and pincers. Pearls and stones are replaceable, and enamel can be repaired, but pieces such as this must be in good working order; spring work can be repaired, but it is extremely costly. Ingenious design and high quality make this Swiss verge watch very collectable.

◄ Mandolin

Form watches in the shapes of musical instruments – in particular the mandolin and harp – were very popular. They were accurate to the smallest detail – this Austrian mandolin form watch even includes gold strings. The movement is set in the sound box, and is invisible when the mandolin is closed, although the balance can be seen through the pearl-set glazed sound hole. The piece is designed to look like a item of jewellery, with an enamelled gold body set with pearls and gold inlay. A spring latch is depressed to reveal the dial and allow the watch to be wound.

Austrian verge, c.1810, signed "Chavanne in Wien", **£4,000–7,000**

1760–1820: repeaters & automatons

The repeating mechanism was developed by Daniel Quare, who, in 1687, patented a single push-piece that sounded the hours and the quarters. Early repeaters employed bells; these were superseded from 1800 by two bent-wire gongs. Many examples striking on a bell had pulse-pieces that silenced the bell but allowed the user to tell the strokes without disturbing other people. Once the mechanism became reliable, the popularity of the repeater pocket watch exploded. Swiss, French, and Austrian watchmakers in particular went further and developed repeaters with automatons, which were common from 1790 to 1830. Articulated figures – "jacquemarts" or "jacks" – were incorporated into a range of novel designs, including much sought-after erotic scenes. Rare and expensive, automatons are a popular collecting niche – the more complicated and original the better.

▼ Quarter repeater with calendar

The elegant silver and gilt consular case of this French cylinder watch may well have been inspired by the silver and gold cases of Breguet. It is an early example of the half-hunter design, in which the solid front case has a glass aperture through which the white enamel dial, with hours, minutes and date, can be seen. The dial has a small chip, but as this would usually be hidden by the half-hunter case it is better left unrestored, as here. The push pendant operates a "dumb" quarter repeater, which strikes on the side of the case to produce a duller sound than on a bell.

French cylinder quarter repeater, c.1780, signed "Fort à Paris", £1,500–3,000

▶ Clockwatch and alarm

The appeal of this watch lies in the superb condition of all the major components: the inner and outer of the silver pair case; a pristine verge movement; and a white enamel dial with gold beetle and poker hands. It has three trains: one to wind the watch; one to wind the clockwatch and repeater mechanism; and one to wind the alarm, which was set by rotating the blued-steel alarm hand. Such good condition is rare, but most watches can at least be cleaned; restored or badly repaired movements are not so easily put right.

English verge clockwatch with alarm, hallmarked London 1790, signed "Spencer & Perkins London 9515", £5,000–8,000

• Repeaters come in hour, quarter hour, half-quarter hour (seven-and-a-half-minute), five-minute, and one-minute versions; they must be in full working order.
• Turn hands clockwise only on repeating alarms or clockwatches.
• Automaton watches must be complete and in working order.
• Musical, erotic, and skeletonized automaton watches are the most collectable.

Swiss verge quarter repeater, c.1810, unsigned, **£5,000–8,000**

Swiss verge quarter repeater automaton, c.1810, signed "Du Chene & Fils", **£5,000–7,000**

French verge quarter repeating automaton, c.1810, unsigned, **£10,000–15,000**

▲ Quarter repeater automaton

This silver Swiss repeater has a rare automaton with gilt repoussé decoration. The two cupids on either side of the pillars strike the quarters; the silver push pendant activates two extra figures – a Father Time and a jester – who appear in the aperture at the top of the dial to strike the hours and then disappear. All four figures are still in working order – an essential part of the value of the watch. It also has a silver open-face case. Silver cases of this type of watch were often made of heavier gauge than their softer gold counterparts; they wear better, and tend to be found in better condition. As a consequence, there is little difference between the prices of silver- and gold-cased automaton watches.

▲ Skeletonized gold repeater

The finely skeletonized dial plate of this gold Swiss watch allows the quarter repeating mechanism to be clearly seen. Skeletonized watches are very popular, and this feature can double the value of a watch. On this example, two Classical gilt figures appear to strike the hours on the decorative bells. Typical Swiss features include the engine turning – at which the Swiss excelled – on the back of the case, and a gilt metal *cuvette*: a piece of metal that hinges onto the inner bezel and protects the mechanism from dust (it was cut to size to fit the Swiss *ébauche* movements). Both of these mechanized techniques allowed the Swiss to assemble watches more quickly and more cheaply.

▲ Automaton with erotic scene

The high value of this French quarter repeater is a result of the good condition of the movement (seen here) and a hidden extra: a repoussé gilt cover underneath the chapter reveals two amorous figures whose couplings match the number of hours being struck! Such erotic automaton watches are rare, highly popular and very valuable; they were nearly all of Swiss and French origin.

1820–50: ladies' watches

During this period Swiss watchmakers came to the fore, producing all types of watch for a wide range of markets and adding calendars, perpetual calendars, musical and automaton features. After the death of Breguet in 1823, French watchmaking entered a relatively stagnant period. English watchmakers concentrated on technical developments, experimenting with the vast range of new escapements – various types of chronometer, lever, and duplex. The patent that was awarded in 1820 to Thomas Prest (*c*.1770–1855) for an early keyless winding system resulted in the perpetual (self-winding) watch. As improved technology made watches smaller and more wearable they became more attractive to women, and it became common for the lady of the house, as well as the master, to have her own watch or watches.

▶ **Gem-set gold case**
Ladies' watches of this period often blur the distinction between jewellery and horology, and they are sought after by collectors of both. Three-colour gold forms the basis for the decoration of this attractive watch. On the open-face case the three-colour gold appears in a foliate pattern, set with turquoise and rubies, on a matt ground. The dial is engine-turned gold, with three-colour gold applied decoration at its edge. Overall condition with watches such as this is important; removing the scratches on an engine-turned gold dial will always damage the decoration itself.

Swiss verge, *c*.1810, signed "Fres Esquillion à Geneve", **£800–2,500**

Austrian verge, *c*.1820, signed "Conrad Kreizer", **£4,000–20,000**

▼ **Rock-crystal crucifix**
A fine example of Austrian ingenuity and construction, this crucifix form watch is probably a copy of a 17thC piece. The silver-gilt, enamel and faceted rock-crystal case and *cloisonné* enamel dial are both in the 17thC style, and the watch even bears a copy of a signature of a well-known 17thC maker, Conrad Kreizer (active c.1600), whose work is found in museums. Whereas a 17thC form watch would only have an hour hand, this one has a minute hand as well, and the motion work has been changed to accommodate it. Nevertheless, the watch has been well cared for, and is highly collectable.

FACT FILE

- Watches made during this period are readily available and reasonably priced, and there is quite a wide choice for collectors.
- Given that the number of watches available is so great, maximum value is conditional on a watch being in very good or excellent condition.
- Good condition is vital, as the original decorative techniques are often difficult and expensive to restore.
- The more elaborate and detailed the decoration, the more desirable the watch, and the greater the cost of restoration.
- Restoration is generally acceptable provided that it does not detract from the visual appeal (enamel watches, in particular, have often been restored).

▼ Gold and enamel shell

Although this example is less ingenious and imposing than the crucifix form watch, the combination of dark-blue enamel and gold in a shape ideally suited to a pendant watch give it the attractive appearance that is the major appeal of ladies' watches. The gold case, in the form of a small shell, is decorated with dark-blue enamel, set with split pearls at the edges, with gold inlay and two gold swans at the corners. Enamel watches are rarely found in perfect condition, but good restoration, such as has been carried out here, will not greatly detract from value as it helps to retain the attractive appearance that makes this watch so desirable.

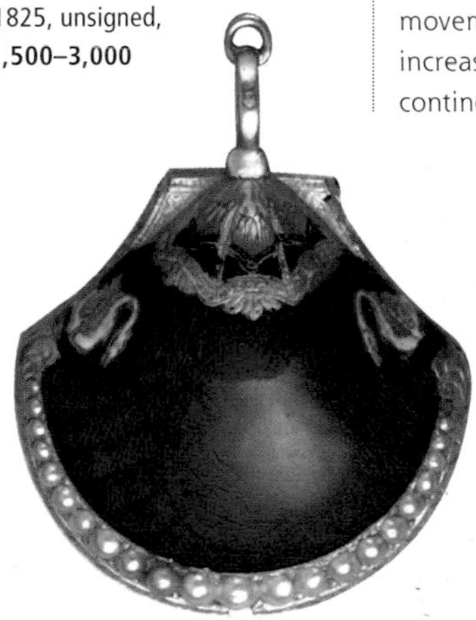

Swiss verge, c.1825, unsigned, **£1,500–3,000**

◄ Gem-set cylinder

This cylinder watch is a good example of Swiss jewellery watchmaking at its best. It is primarily a piece of jewellery rather than a timekeeper, and its appeal lies mainly in the multi-coloured gold back plaque that is set with rubies and emeralds in an attractive design of a vase of flowers. The dial, although clean and clear, is less decorative than might be expected, and the workings are typical of the plain mass-produced durable Swiss movements that were inexpensive to make and maintain. Another interesting feature is the going barrel movement, which became increasingly popular with continental watchmakers.

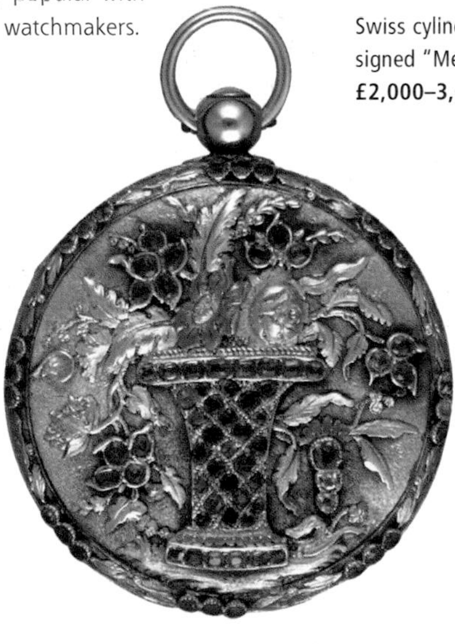

Swiss cylinder, c.1830, signed "Mercier", **£2,000–3,000**

▼ Gold and cloisonné enamel case

The horizontal cylinder escapement enabled makers to produce much slimmer watches, such as this Swiss lady's watch, which is only 8mm (⅓in) deep, including the glass. The decorative blue *cloisonné* enamel on the case is continued onto the front bezel and the pendant and bow. Equally attractive is the Breguet-style engine-turned gold dial with an off-set chapter and Breguet-style "moon" blued-steel hands. Another, less obvious, feature that increases the watch's collectability is the unusual male key, with a stem, which fits into a female winding aperture that is revealed when the back of the watch is rotated a few degrees.

▼ Gold and champlevé enamel case

The pleasing combination of silver dial and gold and champlevé enamel case is the major attraction of this Swiss cylinder watch. The engine-turned dial, with subsidiary seconds, and "moon" hands show the Breguet influence. The gold case, pendant and bow are decorated with black and white champlevé enamel in a striking geometric pattern that sets off the restrained elegance of the dial. However, any damage to such a design would prove very difficult and costly to repair. As is so often the case with watches such as this, an attractive exterior hides an undistinguished, if reliable, semi-mass-produced Swiss movement. The combination of high-quality design and reliable but inexpensive movements allowed the Swiss to produce elegant timepieces at reasonable prices.

Swiss cylinder, *c*.1830, unsigned, £400–1,000

▼ Diamond, gold, and enamel case

This Swiss cylinder watch is a good example of case design following that of contemporary jewellery. The diamond-set foliate design on dark-blue enamel (fully restored) on the back of the 18-carat gold case is typical of that found on pendants and brooches of the period. Watches with pearl-, diamond- or other stone-set designs can be restored, but the new stones must be a perfect match in size, colour, and shape. An attractive dial with Breguet hands adds to the overall appeal.

Swiss cylinder, *c*.1850, signed "S Mercier à Geneve", £500–1,500

Swiss cylinder, *c*.1830, unsigned, £1,500–3,000

French cylinder, c.1850, signed "Marraud & Baugrand Rue de la Paix Paris", £1,700–3,000

▲ Gold and bloodstone pendant watch

Both case and dial are equally stunning on this highly decorative French pendant cylinder watch. The technique used to combine bloodstone (a type of agate) and gems is a very difficult one, and watches in which the two are found are rare and valuable. On the back of the case the bloodstone is combined with gold wire, diamonds, and rubies; the bloodstone dial has diamonds at the five-minute markings and highly unusual roman numerals of white stone inset with black agate – a technique that is sometimes found on French clocks.

A watch of this type must be in good condition; restoration of such a difficult technique would be nearly impossible, and correspondingly costly.

◄ Silver-gilt gem-set form watch

Turquoise and amethysts are combined with silver gilt on this lantern form watch. Form watches are rarely found in silver, and this example would be a very affordable start to a collection, whereas a gold version would cost three times as much. Other attractive features include the original, matching key (collectable in its own right), and the clarity of the small enamel dial. Some of the stones are missing, but, although they could be replaced, they do not detract greatly from the watch's appearance.

FACT FILE

• Although a watch in poor condition may appear to be a bargain, restoration may cost more in the end than a better quality original.
• Clean cases and dials, and original dustcovers suggest that a movement is also well maintained.
• Cases should fit well, while pair cases should be hallmarked with matching dates and maker's initials.
• Attractive appearance is more important than accurate timekeeping.
• Look for watches that combine more than one collectable feature.
• Swiss and French examples are generally most sought after.

Swiss cylinder, c.1850, unsigned, £200–700

1820–50: decorative dials

By this period, engine-turning machinery was readily available, allowing English, French, and Swiss watchmakers to produce attractively engraved cases and dials that were nonetheless inexpensive. Dials that used different colour golds were popular; British makers produced three-colour examples, and combinations of up to six colours were known. White enamel dials were often in the elegant, clear style inspired by Breguet, with distinctive Breguet hands. Polychrome enamel dials were still found, but the subject matter often reflected the increasingly urban and industrial landscape. Early commemorative railway scenes are particularly sought after, as are dials with mottoes or initials, which became even rarer after 1820.

French verge, c.1820, unsigned, £750–1,500

◀ Digital dial
The silver dial of this French verge has fine engine turning, and an off-set regulator section for minutes and subsidiary seconds, while the hours are shown in arabic numerals through the aperture at the top of the dial. Its restrained elegance shows the influence of Breguet, and many French makers of the period strove to emulate the work produced at the famous workshop. Its collecting appeal lies in the good, clean condition of the open-face silver case and dial; the digital dial approximately triples the watch's value.

▼ Breguet repeater
Although not made by Breguet himself, this quarter repeater was almost certainly finished in the famous Breguet workshop in Paris. The elegant, open, clear white enamel dial has a tiny signature – "Breguet à Paris" – beneath the roman numeral VI and characteristic Breguet hands in fine gold. Although the inner gilt *cuvette* is original, the engine-turned silver and gilt open-face case, while contemporary, is a replacement, which reduces the overall value by about 40 per cent. Full restoration, as here, is acceptable on unpainted enamel dials.

French cylinder, c.1820, signed "Breguet à Paris", £750–2,000

English Massey lever, hallmarked London 1825, signed "John Moncas Liverpool 4407", **£600–1,200**

▶ **Three-colour gold dial**

Three-colour gold dials, as seen on this English Massey lever watch, were a popular feature at this time. The engine-turned centre, with a subsidiary seconds dial, is surrounded by an applied three-colour gold decorative border with applied gold numerals. The excellent condition of the dial is not quite matched by that of the 18-carat gold case, where the engine turning around the deeply chased and engraved middle is slightly faded. It is, however, the original case, as the number on it matches that on the movement.

◀ **Motto dial**

The rather mundane silver pair cases of this English verge watch conceal a very attractive three-piece dial. Made of gilt metal, with a white enamel chapter and engraved metal centre, the outer metal ring is inscribed "Keep me clean and treat me well and I to you the truth will tell". This advice was often found on watchpapers (themselves collectable) placed inside the outer case, but to see it on the dial is rare. The movement was made in the north of England and the case in Birmingham, a sign that by this period the watchmaking industry was moving out of London.

English verge, hallmarked Birmingham 1826, signed "Thos Holmes Cheadle 786", **£300–600**

- Decorative dials are well suited to thematic collections; popular areas include English painted dials, historical dials that celebrate events such as military and naval victories or technological developments such as railway transport, Masonic dials, and specialized dials such as those produced for the Chinese and Turkish export markets.
- Quality of painting will determine the value of a dial. English and French makers in particular are noted for their expertise; Dutch makers tended to imitate English styles.
- The painted decoration on polychrome enamel dials should not be restored unless it is very badly damaged; minor flaws such as hairline cracks are acceptable.

▼ Personalized dial

Dials on which the owner's name replaces numerals were never common, but they were exceptionally rare after 1820, which makes this silver English fusee watch very collectable. The slight damage to the dial – hairline cracks – and minor restoration – a repaired chip – are infinitely preferable to full restoration, which might cast doubt on the authenticity of the dial; they do, however, reduce the watch's value by some 50 per cent. The fusee lever movement was more common from the mid-1820s, but although this example has been elegantly signed, it no longer features the decorative engraving and piercing found on earlier watches.

English fusee lever, hallmarked London 1837, signed "Alex Purvis 4 North Audley Street Grosvenor Squ London 4152", **£200–500**

▼ Engine-turned dial

This silver dial, with its profuse foliate engraving at the centre and applied gold roman numerals, is typical of English engine-turned dials of the period. Good condition is essential as it is impossible to polish out scratches on the dial without damaging or removing the engine turning at the same time. The silver full-hunter case is substantial but is missing a fly spring to the front cover. Ideally, case springs should be complete and undamaged as they are very expensive to restore. The standard verge movement has been left unsigned, which was a common practice at the time; the movement was often left blank so that the jewellery retailer, rather than the watchmaker, was able to add his or her signature.

▼ Polychrome enamel dial

The beginning of the railway is the unusual theme pictured on this very rare polychrome dial. The foreground depicts a canal barge being drawn by a horse; the horse is rearing in fright as a train with three carriages passes behind it. Similar early railway scenes are found on other watches produced by the same maker – C. Bullingford – and all hallmarked within a four-year period, which suggests that he may have been specially commissioned by one of the early railway companies. The dial has a small chip at its centre, but any restoration of the painted scene would reduce the value of the watch dramatically.

English verge, hallmarked Birmingham 1840, signed "C Bullingford London", **£700–1,500**

English verge, hallmarked London 1837, unsigned, **£150–300**

- Restoration of a plain white enamel dial is acceptable if it has been well executed, but ensure that the dial is original and not a cheaply overpainted substitute.
- Engine-turned dials must be in good condition, as scratches cannot be polished out without damaging the decoration; digital dials are rarer and therefore more valuable.
- Early commemorative railway, industrial, and sporting scenes are particularly sought after.
- Personalized dials are rare after 1820 and very collectable.

▲ ▶ Gold digital dial

This deceptively slim French cylinder watch contains a few surprises. The elaborate black and polychrome enamel decoration on the hunter case continues onto the unusual gold digital dial, which has two small apertures for hours and minutes. The scalloped enamel border on the front cover has a matching border, set with diamonds, on the back cover, and this frames a portrait of a demure young girl. However, beneath this cover is concealed an erotic scene in which a far from demure young woman is enjoying the attentions of a young man. The digital dial, concealed erotic scene, overall attractiveness, and good condition of this watch contribute to its high value.

French cylinder, c.1840, signed "Bouchet à Paris", **£5,000–12,000**

▶ Chinese export cylinder

The company of Bovet Fleurier was one of the best-known (and is now one of the most collectable) Swiss makers of watches for the Chinese export market between 1822 and 1864. This particular example has a white card dial, with roman numerals on the inner chapter and Chinese markings and centre seconds on the outer. The card dial is probably a replacement for a damaged original enamel dial, which would have been difficult to repair in China. The unusual polished-steel keywind bar movement has a suspended going barrel.

Swiss cylinder, c.1840, signed "Bovet Fleurier", **£200–600**

1820–50: technical developments

During this period, watchmakers were inventing and perfecting many new and existing types of escapement in their search for more reliable and accurate timekeepers that would require a minimum of maintenance. Collectors, therefore, have a wide range of individual escapements from which to choose. The cylinder escapement had been developed to its limit and was now mass-produced and available in steel or ruby versions. Ultimately it was to be replaced by the less complicated and more durable lever escapement in its many forms. Work continued on the chronometer, while calendars, perpetual calendars, musical, and automaton watches were all produced and are popular collecting areas today, together with unusual escapements and variations on the lever.

▶ Rack lever

Morris Tobias (1794–1840), one of the best-known makers of his time, worked in Liverpool before moving to London and then to the USA. This full-plate gilt keywind fusee movement by him has an unusual rack lever escapement with a large 30-toothed brass escape wheel. The subsidiary seconds hand is mounted on its arbor end and rotates four times a minute in 15-second cycles; matching pair cases bear the maker's initials and the stamp "T & Co 5235". The movement, however, is numbered "5236", which seems to suggest either that two identical watches were produced, the cases of which came to be transposed accidentally, or that perhaps a clerical error was made.

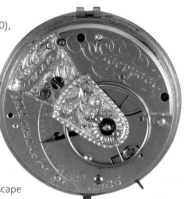

English rack lever, hallmarked Chester 1820, signed "M I Tobias & Co Liverpool 5236", £600–900

▼ English cylinder

An English cylinder movement typical of its period, this watch also has an unusual six-spoke pierced and engraved round cock with a diamond endstone. The polished-steel cylinder has a large brass escape wheel. It is important that a watch with a brass escape wheel should be in working order and running correctly, as brass wheels are often badly worn and likely to prove expensive to restore. Cylinder escapements are not noted for their accuracy, and may gain or lose 15 minutes a day. This collectable movement is housed in a purpose-made engine-turned case that is hallmarked "1858" – some 30 years after the movement was made.

English cylinder, c.1825, signed "Thompson Bath", £150–300

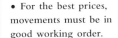

▼ French cylinder

The appeal of this silver French cylinder watch is that it combines several collectable features – a movement typical of its time, a quality case, and an interesting dial – in one timepiece. The keywind Lepine calibre movement, introduced by J.A. Lepine c.1770, was reliable, of simple construction, and easy to maintain; it also dispensed with the top plate, making it possible to produce much slimmer watches. By this time continental watches had adopted the English tradition of winding through the back. This watch, with its slim profile and silver off-set engine-turned dial (see also p.32 for the very similar "Digital dial") emulates the style of the pieces made in the famous Breguet workshop.

French cylinder, c.1830, unsigned, **£900–1,500**

▼ Duplex hunter

The crab-tooth duplex was the escapement most commonly used on watches for export to China. Invented by C.E. Jacot in 1830, it is named after the doubled teeth on the escape wheel, which look like crabs' claws; this example, which has a large symmetrical bridge, is unusually clean, contributing to the value. The white enamel dial is typical of watches that were intended for the Chinese market, and has gold hands. The engine-turned silver full-hunter case is slightly rubbed, but this is far preferable to overzealous restoration.

Swiss crab-tooth duplex, c.1840, signed "Girard London", **£500–1,500**

English lever, hallmarked Birmingham 1841, signed "Matt Ord Hexham 204", **£100–300**

- For the best prices, movements must be in good working order.
- Check for worn brass wheels that will lead to irregular timekeeping and are difficult to restore.
- Cylinder escapements tend to be unreliable, and may gain or lose 10 to 15 minutes a day.
- Unusual movements are sought after: ruby cylinders, chronometers, levers by Savage (d.1855) and Massey (1772–1852), and duplex.
- An unusual cock adds to collectability.
- Tobias watches were faked by Swiss makers and exported to the USA; check for second-rate movements and inappropriate cases.

▼ Fusee lever

Subsidiary seconds were a standard feature by this time. This watch also has a lateral steel stop lever that could stop and start the seconds feature, allowing the watch to be used as a stopwatch. The problem with this feature was that the whole movement stopped as well, with the consequent loss of accuracy. The typical English table-roller lever escapement is in excellent condition but is lacking its dustcover – this is quite common and does not detract greatly from value.

1850–1950: decorative watches

This period saw the development of the inexpensive mass-produced pocket watch. The small workshop was replaced by watchmaking companies that employed up to 40 or 50 watchmakers and often bought in Swiss *ébauche* movements that were refined and finished in house. The Swiss reputation for watchmaking was upheld by companies such as Vacheron & Constantin (est.1819), Audemar (est.1840; later Audemar Piguet), and Patek Philippe (est.1845), while American firms developed inexpensive "customized" watches made from different combinations of movements and cases. Faced with increasing competition from the wristwatch (largely the consequence of World War I; *see* p.48), and from each other, pocket-watch manufacturers developed a range of novel features in order to boost dwindling sales.

▼ Crab-tooth duplex

Crab-tooth duplex movements, in this case heavily engraved and decorated, were standard on watches made for export to China, as were centre seconds. The engraved gilt full-hunter case, however, opens to reveal a far from typical polychrome dial. It features a charming and unusual painted clock, the face of which is formed by a small enamel watch dial. There is also a mock pendulum bob that moves when the watch is running.

Swiss crab-tooth duplex, c.1860, unsigned, £750–1,500

▼ Red-gold lever

This Swiss lever is modelled on the consular-cased pocket watch of the early 18thC, but possesses features associated with 19thC mass-production. The white enamel dial has the clarity of contemporary dials, while the subsidiary second dial was more common in the 19thC. Although it is mass-produced the movement is of fine quality and has the compensation balance developed in the 1850s. The case is red-gold case, which is preferred by European collectors to yellow gold.

Swiss lever, c.1880, unsigned, £450–1,200

- Mass-production led to standardization, and the precision of watches tends to take precedence over decoration.
- Less expensive mass-produced watches were considered disposable – many were thrown away, so fewer are available than might be expected.
- Gunmetal, nickel (plated), platinum, stainless steel, steel, and white gold were added to the range of materials used for watch cases.
- Features that do more that simply tell the time add to collectability, but they must be in good working order – it is important to check before purchase.

Swiss lever, c.1880, signed "Ivel", **£750–1,500**

▲ Double-sided calendar

A double-sided watch poses a problem: how to look at just one dial at a time. One solution, utilized by this Swiss lever watch, was to adjust the position of the bow on the pendant to choose which one of the gold hunter lids to open. The signed front white enamel dial shows hours and minutes and has a subsidiary seconds dial, while the back dial (which can be seen here) is a day/date calendar; both have gold hands. Any feature over and above simple time-telling will increase a watch's collectability, but it must be in working condition in order to achieve maximum value.

Swiss lever, c.1880, unsigned, **£350–750**

▲ Double-sided calendar

Two dials make this Swiss lever unusual and highly collectable. The front dial has a central cutout to show the phases of the moon; the back dial (seen here) shows the days of the week, the month, and the date. Non-reflective gunmetal cases were first seen c.1870 and became increasingly common, especially in military watches. Gunmetal cases, such as this, must be in good condition, with no rust, and with most of the original bluing present.

▼ Flyback hand

An unusual dial and a flyback hand set this Swiss lever watch apart. The silvered metal dial has a small aperture beneath the 12 o'clock position, inside which a small silver disc shows the hours, with a subsidiary seconds dial above six o'clock. The minutes at the top of the dial are indicated by a hand that flies back when it reaches 60. This mechanism must be tested before buying, as it would be very difficult to repair. A metal dial in mint condition might be worth up to three times as much as a scruffy one.

Swiss lever, c.1885, signed "Modernasta Patent", **£300–700**

▼ Digital dial

The good clean condition of the dial, movement, and case of this silver Swiss lever watch are essential to its value. The double digital dial has fine gilt floral decoration around the edge, a circular aperture for the hours, and a sector-shaped aperture for the minutes above a subsidiary seconds dial. The accuracy of the working mechanism can be checked by setting the watch at five minutes to the hour to check that the hours click forward as the 60-minute mark passes. A similar movement and design in gold would prove considerably more expensive.

Swiss lever, c.1900, signed "Sandoz Boucherin", £350–1,500

▼ Photograph frame watch

Swiss ingenuity in producing unusual designs to boost sales is evinced by this keyless lever watch movement set in a silver and enamel photograph frame. The signed white enamel dial has floral decoration and is set in an easel photograph frame to create a timepiece that is decorative and functional. Novel combinations such as this are an interesting addition to any collection of unusual 20thC watches.

Swiss lever, c.1920, signed "Juvenia Fab. Suisse", £500–800

▼ Masonic watch

Masonic watches of this type were made from c.1900 to c.1940. Earlier watches, such as this one, have the more desirable mother-of-pearl dials that were replaced by enamel versions on later examples. Masonic symbols replace numerals on the dial and are engraved on the back of the gilt metal case, which hinges open to form an easel stand. Gold cases are rarer and more expensive than silver or gilt-metal versions. It is important that mother-of-pearl dials are undamaged, as restoration is always visible.

Swiss lever, c.1920, signed "Solvil Watch Co. 15 jewels 3 Adj Swiss", £1,300–1,700

▼ Lapis lazuli and steel case

A typical Art Deco combination of lapis lazuli and steel makes a highly attractive case for this Swiss lever watch. This example is signed "Tiffany & Co" – the American retailer often bought in movements from leading Swiss manufacturers for use in its own cases. The bevelled lapis lazuli is still in excellent condition; this is an essential prerequisite for maximum value, as the stone cannot be repaired. Art Deco watches often followed contemporary jewellery styles, which makes them equally appealing to collectors of watches and of Art Deco pieces in general. The fact that the watch has a famous and collectable retailer is a bonus.

◄ Table-lighter watch

Cigarettes were an essential accessory during the "Jazz Age" of the 1920s and 1930s, and manufacturers were swift to capitalize with a range of refined table lighters with integral watches. Made in France, this Art Deco silvered petrol lighter has engine turning on the back, and a silvered dial with gilt arabic numerals and gilt hands on the front; it is driven by an eight-day Swiss twin-barrel movement. Both watch and lighter must be in working order for maximum value.

Swiss lever, c.1930, signed "Tiffany & Co", **£1,000–3,000**

Swiss twin barrel, c.1930, signed "Lancel Automatique", **£100–1,000**

1850–1950: precision watches

By the end of the 19thC verge and cylinder escapements had become rare – watchmakers tended to focus on the lever movement. Precision and accuracy were the aim. There were refinements to the regulation of the hairspring, with the introduction of palladium and other metals. Shock-absorbing technology was improved and used increasingly, as were waterproofing and self-winding. A deck watch or ship's chronometer is an essential part of any collection of precision watches from this period. Split-second chronographs are sought after, as are pocket chronometers, calendars (especially perpetual calendars), and all types of repeaters.

▼ Fusee chronometer

The reasonable price of this fine English fusee chronometer is due to the fact that it is no longer housed in its original case. A later, silver, open-face American case, even though it is well fitted, detracts from the overall value, and offers the collector of movements the chance to buy a genuine bargain.

The movement is a keywind fusee and chain, with a freesprung helical hairspring and an Earnshaw-type spring detent chronometer escapement; the white enamel dial is signed "Chronometer 1784". This example was made in Lancashire, which was one of the many new centres for English watch production.

English fusee chronometer, c.1870, signed "Gardner Manchester", £300–500

▼ Quarter repeater

This Swiss quarter repeater combines subsidiaries for the day, date, month, and seconds with a moon-phase indicator and a centre seconds flyback chronograph. The dial is in excellent condition, while the replacement 14-carat gold hunter case is purpose-made. The brass replacement bezel could easily be changed for a gold one and does not greatly reduce the watch's value. The repeater is operated by a slide mechanism that is preferable to the push thumbpiece found on lower-quality examples.

Swiss club foot lever with quarter repeater, c.1880, unsigned, £1,700–3,000

English lever with half-quarter repeater, hallmarked London 1873, signed "Upjohn Bright & Wood 15 King William Strt Strand London", **£1,700–3,500**

▲ Half-quarter repeater

As well the quarter hours, this English lever repeater can also strike the half quarter (every seven-and-a-half minutes). This unusual and rare feature is found in conjunction with a substantial 18-carat gold half-hunter case, with a blue enamel chapter ring, and an attractive signed white enamel dial with subsidiary seconds. The repeater strikes on two polished-steel gongs and is activated by a gold slide lever. It is important to check that both the repeater feature and the slide that operates it are working properly before buying a watch of this type.

▼ Quarter-repeater automaton

In the late 19thC Swiss makers produced automaton watches that were very popular at the time and remain so today with collectors. This example has a multi-coloured enamel dial and two jacquemarts who strike the bells above them when the repeater mechanism sounds. There is an unusually fine keyless bar movement with going barrel, compensation balance, and gold train wheels. The high quality of the dial, movement, and 18-carat gold full-hunter case are reflected in the price.

Swiss lever automaton with quarter repeater, c.1885, signed "Gme Hoffe et Fils Chaux de Fonds", **£5,000–10,000**

Swiss lever automaton with quarter repeater, c.1880, signed "Le Coultre", **£3,500–5,000**

▲ Quarter-repeater automaton

The Swiss company Le Coultre (est.1849) was one of the best manufacturers of the period, although this watch is not one of its finest. Nevertheless it is collectable, with its repeater mechanism and automaton; when the repeater mechanism is activated by a gold slide, the winged figure and the top putto appear to strike the bell.

1850–1950: everyday watches

The expansion of the watch industries in Europe and the USA made their product increasingly affordable. In Switzerland, Georges-Frédéric Roskopf (1813–89) founded a new low-priced watchmaking industry that produced an everyday pocket watch costing just 20 Swiss francs, and in the USA in 1896 the brothers Robert and Charles Ingersoll bought a pocket watch from the Waterbury Watch Company that they sold through mail order for one dollar – pocket watches were now within the range of most people. Collectors search for typical examples that are still in excellent condition. Although many thousands of watches were manufactured, their reasonable prices meant that they were increasingly regarded as expendable and easily replaceable. Good clean condition is essential, as is a working movement.

◀ **English chronograph**
A typical English chronograph of the period, this large pocket watch is in excellent working condition. The silver open-face case has engine turning, slightly rubbed at the edge, and an empty cartouche on the back cover. The clear white enamel dial has a blued-steel second hand with a stop/start facility that is activated by a gold thumbpiece in the band. Although popular, this feature, by stopping the whole movement, could greatly reduce a watch's accuracy.

Swiss lever, c.1865, signed "Patek Philippe & Cie Geneve 24094", £1,000–3,000

English chronograph, hallmarked Birmingham 1865, signed "J Harris Wolverhampton", £100–300

▼ **Patek Philippe lever**
Such is the renown of the Swiss company Patek Philippe (est.1845) that its signature, rather than the quality of the movement, will often determine a watch's value. This pocket watch has a signed dial; the movement, however, despite being typical of Patek Philippe, is unsigned, as was the norm with movements during this time. Later Patek Philippe models (those made after c.1880) possess three signatures: on the movement, case and dial. Although there are better examples of Swiss open-face pocket watches to be found, this is a relatively modest piece by a famous and sought-after maker.

▼ Half-hunter case

Edward John Dent (1790–1853) was the founder of the London company that would become Watchmaker to Queen Victoria and design "Big Ben". Dent (est.1840) was a leading British company of the period, and in addition to the famous signature on the dial this gold half-hunter lever has another feature typical of the firm: a subsidiary second dial set at nine o'clock rather than at six o'clock. This was also typical of Adolphe Nicole (active mid-19thC), an English maker who supplied the firms of Dent and Frodsham, which then sold his watches under their own names. The hour hand has the double-spade ends typical of half-hunter watches, which allowed the wearer to tell the hour through the small glass aperture without opening the case.

▼ Swiss cylinder

Although it is a standard and common pocket watch, the excellent overall condition of this small gold Swiss cylinder provides the major appeal for collectors. The small 18-carat gold open-face case has a chased and engraved middle and bezels on the front dial, an engraved harbour scene on the back, and a signed gold *cuvette*. Being in near mint condition almost doubles the watch's value, making it a highly desirable long-term investment against the day when watches such as this become rare.

Swiss cylinder, c.1870, signed "Racine Geneve", £100–500

- Good condition may double the value of an everyday watch.
- Watches by renowned European makers such as Frodsham (est.1834), Dent, and Patek Philippe are sought after.
- *Cuvette* and dial are signed and/or numbered on Patek Philippe watches made before c.1875; after c.1880, the movement, case, and dial were all signed.
- Highly sought–after American pocket watches include Waltham's 19- and 21-jewel "Riverside", "Riverside Maximus", and "Vanguard"; and Hamilton's "992", "992B", and "49920".

▼ Hamilton "992B"

Hamilton's "992B" pocket watch's high-grade movement features a "992" micrometer regulator, 21 jewels, and a rolled-gold open-face case. The railroad dial has black arabic numerals and red five-minute markings. One of the most desirable of American pocket watches, the example seen here is even more valuable as it comes complete with its original signed box.

American lever, c.1942, signed "Hamilton Watch Co. USA 992B 21 Jewels Adj. Temp and 6 positions", £200–400

English lever, hallmarked London 1868, signed "Dent Watchmaker to the Queen 61 Strand and 34 Royal Exchange London 33797", £750–1,500

1850–1950: ladies' watches

The market for ladies' watches and jewellery watches was now firmly established. Swiss and French makers continued to lead the field, but American makers swiftly joined them towards the turn of the century, with well-known names such as Tiffany retailing exclusive and highly collectable watches. During the 1920s and 1930s, the Art Deco style influenced a range of sophisticated, glamorous, and, today, collectable watches that appeal equally to horologists and to Art Deco aficionados. Such watches are primarily pieces of jewellery, and their appeal will be determined by their appearance rather than accurate timekeeping; condition, therefore, is important, and restoration is acceptable only if it is in keeping with the original design and enhances attractiveness.

American lever, c.1865, signed "P J Bartlett Waltham Mss Foggs Safety Pinion Pat Feb 14 1865", **£400–1,000**

◀ **Gold and enamel lever**
The virtually mint condition of this American gold and enamel lever has certainly doubled its value. The 18-carat gold full-hunter case is profusely engraved and decorated with black champlevé enamel in a foliate pattern. The original, unrestored decoration on the case, an unrestored white enamel dial, and the original gold *cuvette* make it a highly desirable example of an early American lady's watch, and it would be a good addition to a collection of either ladies' or American watches.

▶ **Gilt-metal chatelaine**
The chatelaine, which was a rare feature by this time, is the main attraction of this English watch, while the keywind fusee lever watch is a bonus. Although the open-face case is of 18-carat gold and lavishly carved, the chatelaine, which has a brooch pin, is of gilt metal, as are the glazed protective outer case and the dial. Such a late example will appeal to collectors of chatelaines and of ladies' watches alike.

English fusee lever, c.1874, unsigned, **£350–1,000**

Swiss cylinder, c.1880,
unsigned, £800–1,200

Swiss cylinder, c.1880, signed
"London & Ryde 17 New Bond
Street London", £2,500–4,000

▲ Fob watch

Polychrome enamel decoration
hasn't lost its appeal, despite
being particularly vulnerable
and usually requiring some
degree of restoration. On
this Swiss cylinder lady's fob
watch, the polychrome scene
of two doves in a green
enamel frame has been fully
restored, but the restoration is
so well executed that it does
not detract from the watch's
overall value. The open-face
case is 18-carat gold, chased
and engraved, and the dial
has further gilt decoration in
the centre and around the
border. This combination of
gold, gilt, and polychrome
enamel decoration, and good
condition, is typical of the
high-quality enamel watches
Swiss makers were producing
during this period.

▲ Miniature pendant

At 15.8mm (⅝in) in diameter,
this very rare Swiss cylinder
is reputedly the smallest
keywind pendant watch ever
made, which explains its high
value. The white enamel dial
has hairline cracks, but the
open-face 18-carat gold case
is in excellent condition, and
is attached to a diamond-set
gold brooch. Although made
in Switzerland, it was retailed
by the English firm of London
& Ryde of Bond Street.

▼ Tiffany pendant

The case and famous Tiffany
signature transform this lady's
pendant watch from a Swiss
lever of little horological merit
into a highly desirable piece
of jewellery. The silvered dial,
signed "Tiffany & Co New
York", is set in an octagonal
gold case, with bezels that are
decorated with bands of white
and translucent blue enamel
on an engine-turned ground.
On the back case, a glass
intaglio of a cupid
is surrounded by a
diamond-set frame
with matching
diamond-set
small clip.

Swiss lever,
c.1895, signed
"Tiffany & Co
New York",
£2,000–
5,000

Wristwatches: before 1930

Although produced as early as *c.*1850, wristwatches didn't really capture the horological market until the end of the 19thC. German naval officers were being supplied with Swiss wristwatches by 1880, and, some seven years later, English ladies out hunting were wearing small Swiss pendant watches strapped to their wrists in leather cases. Growing industrialization, increasing mass production, and the development of the railway system all contributed to a faster pace of life that fuelled the need for a reliable portable timepiece, and in the trenches during World War I the advantages of having a watch strapped to the wrist rather than in a pocket became obvious – the wristwatch was in the ascendancy.

▶ Nickel export watch

The Swiss company Longines (est.1866) produced this nickel watch for a Turkish retailer in Constantinople, and their joint signatures appear on the white enamel dial. The arabic numerals are luminous – quite a common feature from c.1890 – and the original hands were probably also luminous, but such hands are fragile and are often replaced on being damaged, as they have been here. Hinged lugs, good overall condition, and a well-known manufacturer make this an interesting piece dating from very late in the period during which watches were produced specifically for export to Turkey.

Swiss bar lever, c.1913, signed "Longines – Nacib K. Djezvedjian & Son Constantinople 3097471", **£750–1,300**

▼ Silver wristwatch

Although this silver watch has the half-hunter-style case usually associated with pocket watches, the position of the dial and close inspection of the lugs reveal it to be purpose-made and not a less desirable conversion. Luminous numerals and the original luminous "spider" hands, combined with a protective cover, suggest that this is an early military watch – a popular collecting niche. An unusual feature is the push-button opening facility below the subsidiary seconds dial.

Swiss bar with going barrel, hallmarked London 1917, unsigned, **£300–400**

Swiss club foot lever, *c.*1920, signed "Longines", £750–2,000

▼ Czech pilot's watch

These Swiss steel watches were mass-produced for the military. A non-reflective black enamel dial with luminous hands is set in a sturdy "cushion-shape" steel case. The dial is signed "Longines", and the back of the watch carries the imprint of the Czechoslovakian airforce. The excellent overall condition is so rare as to suggest that this example was never issued, remaining, instead, in storage. Early military watches are sought after, and those that are unrestored and in almost mint condition are worth two or three times as much as less well-preserved pieces.

▲ Art Deco-style watch

Although contemporary with the Czech pilot's watch (left), and by the same maker, this Longines lady's watch could not be more different in style. It is primarily collectable as a piece of jewellery, and the geometrical rectangular design anticipates the Art Deco style that became so fashionable. The gold case is enhanced by the design of sapphires and diamonds that continues onto the hinged lugs. A silvered dial, as seen here, can be restored quite inexpensively, and a damaged glass was often replaced with perspex.

- Many original ladies' pendant watches had their pendants removed and replaced by lugs; such "conversions" are difficult to spot, and, if there is any doubt, ask for written confirmation of authenticity.
- Movements must be running and accurate.
- Clean, unrestored dials are most desirable.
- Watches by important makers are highly priced and sought after. Rolex, Cartier, Patek Philippe, and Audemar Piguet (est.1875) watches are faked; check carefully, and seek professional advice if necessary.
- Purpose-made wristwatches are more desirable than pocket-watch conversions.

▼ Gold, enamel, and diamond watch suite

This gold and enamel lady's watch is a very rare example of the transition from pendant to wristwatch. The ingenious design allows the gold, enamel, and diamond-set case to be worn as a ring, bracelet, choker or brooch on an 18-carat gold band, expanding bracelet and black silk strap respectively. The watch's appeal is its design rather than any horological merit that it might possess.

Swiss lever calibre 15.94, *c.*1920, signed "Longines 3940802", £350–1,100

Swiss lever, *c.*1925, signed "Rotherhams", £3,500–4,500

Wristwatches: 1930–45

While much of Europe struggled with the war effort, Switzerland's neutrality allowed Swiss companies to dominate wristwatch production, winning huge contracts for mass-produced troop-issue watches. Famous names such as Audemar Piguet, Patek Philippe, International Watch Company (or IWC; est.1868), and Rolex (est.1908) consolidated their European reputations, while America was catered for by indigenous manufacturers such as Waltham (est.1857) and Hamilton (est.1874). As the 20thC progressed, watches became increasingly accurate, more dustproof, and ever easier to maintain. Favoured materials included platinum and white gold – both now rare and sought after – and steel for the military watches that have become so popular with collectors.

▶ Steel duodial

The geometrical lines associated with Art Deco are echoed here by the use of black and gilt batons rather than numerals on this wristwatch by Longines. The signed dial is virtually divided into two (hence "duodial"), with hours and minutes in the top half and subsidiary seconds in the bottom half. Superb overall condition, and matching numbers on the steel case and calibre 9.32 lever movement, contribute to making this a highly desirable example of the typical high-quality Swiss-produced watches of the period.

Swiss lever calibre 9.32, c.1931, signed "Longines 5234441", **£1,000–2,000**

▼ Two-tone dial

The excellent condition of the elegant gilt and silver two-tone dial on this Swiss watch plays a large part in its value, as two-colour restoration is both difficult and expensive. The steel case has the fashionable rectangular shape, echoed in the dial and subsidiary dial, with a smart black crocodile strap. In general, straps do not affect value as they are easy to replace, although it is always worth keeping the original buckle if the maker is well known.

Swiss 15-jewel lever, c.1936, signed "Omega", **£150–600**

▼ IWC platinum watch

Platinum was a popular material during this period; on this watch it has been used for the tonneau-shaped case and the applied numerals and batons on the silvered dial. A watch in platinum will be rarer and more expensive than a similar example in a different metal, but the high value of this watch can also be attributed to a well-known maker and excellent overall condition. The original sale certificate is still extant, as is a bill for overhauling by IWC. Proof of work by a reputable company such as IWC will add some 30 per cent to value.

Swiss lever calibre 87, c.1938, signed "International Watch Co. Schaffhausen 1010049", **£3,000–6,000**

Swiss 15-jewel lever, c.1940, signed "Cyma", **£150–500**

▲ Unused vintage watch

Some 80 per cent of the value of this standard Swiss steel wristwatch can be attributed to the fact that it was bought from unsold stock and has not been used. The steel case, steel clip-on back, signed silvered dial with unusual reverse-dart gold hands, and 15-jewel signed movement are all in mint condition. Watches such as this are at a premium, and, although usually expensive, should hold their value.

Swiss lever, c.1945, signed "National Watch", **£350–1,250**

• All subsidiary horological features should be in accurate working order.
• Try to retain all original sales material and details of restoration work or overhauling. Not only will these become the watch papers of tomorrow, but proof that a quality overhaul has been undertaken can also add considerably to a watch's value.
• Good condition is of paramount importance; complex dials in particular cannot be easily restored.
• Any watch in clean condition should hold its value.
• Platinum and white-gold watches are rare and collectable.

▼ Steel chronograph

This typical circular steel case with large flexible lugs houses a complex silvered telemeter dial. Luckily the signed dial is in good condition, as it would be very difficult to restore with its continuous subsidiary seconds, flyback centre seconds, and minute recording subsidiary; also of interest is the twin-button chronograph. Such features must be in good working order for maximum value, and the would-be collector should ask to see them operate.

Wristwatches: after 1945

After post-war austerity came the consumer boom. Everyone wanted and expected to have at least one wristwatch in an increasingly time-conscious world. By the time that electronic watches were pioneered in 1957, by Hamilton in the USA, the whole world had become style conscious, and changing one's watch was a matter of course in a disposable, style- and status-driven society. In the 1960s the Swiss developed the quartz watch, with no moving parts; in 1983 the Swatch watch appeared – the ultimate throwaway fashion watch. Meanwhile, at the end of the 1940s, Japanese manufacturers began developing a range of inexpensive and sophisticated mass-produced watches that, today, possess as many as 20 different features. There is, needless to say, a large range for collectors to chose from.

◀ IWC "Mark XI"

This stainless-steel British army issue watch is one of the most collectable of all military watches. Comparatively few were made, and, although issued in Canada and South Africa as well, they are rarely found in such good condition. This one, with black enamel dial and centre seconds, has a "hack" feature: by pulling out the winding stem you could set the watch to the exact second – clearly of value to military personnel. The "Mark XI" is often faked because it is so popular; check that the movement has not been replaced by one without the hack feature, and that the back is original (compare with a watch whose authenticity can be guaranteed).

Swiss club-foot lever, c.1952, signed "International Watch Co Swiss", £1,400–1,800

▼ Bulgari watch

Watches retailed by the Italian company Bulgari (est.1884) are primarily fashion accessories, and are collected for their designer name and style rather than horological merit. Nevertheless, they keep their value as they are not mass-produced, being issued in limited production runs. On this watch the Swiss quartz movement is housed in an 18-carat gold turned case, with a black dial with gilt batons, and the name "Bulgari" prominently displayed on the gold bezel. A characteristic feature is the integrated gold and steel "Tubogas" bracelet, on which the gold clasp can be positioned at will.

Swiss quartz, c.1995, signed "Bulgari Fabrique en Suisse", £2,000–3,500

▼ Japanese lady's watch

The technological skill of Japanese companies such as Seiko – which marketed the first quartz watch – enables them to produce amazingly slim yet reliable circuitry, exemplified by this gold quartz wristwatch at only 1.8mm (0.07in) deep. The 18-carat yellow-gold case has a flat crystal (the glass of the watch), and a gold back; there is a gold Seiko buckle on the crocodile strap. Expensive now, in time these watches, in good condition, will probably be highly sought after as early examples of the sophisticated Japanese technology applied to watchmaking. As with all contemporary watches, keep all display material, bills of sale, and so on – these will be of interest to future collectors, and guarantees of authenticity.

Japanese quartz, 1993, signed "Seiko", £750–1,500

Quartz, c.1996, £15–60

▲ Watch cufflinks

Designers have come up with some ingenious responses to the challenge posed by small, compact movements. Here, quartz movements have been set in a pair of gilt cufflinks (with a diameter of 24mm or 1in), which allows the globe-trotting executive to set each cufflink to a different time zone, and to make sure that his right hand knows what his left is doing! It is difficult to know how appealing future generations of collectors will find such adaptations, but if the intriguing watch suite that was seen earlier (see p.49) is anything to go by, it would appear that inventiveness is never out of fashion.

- Keep display material, guarantees, sales receipts, and so on, as proofs of authenticity and for future interest.
- Modern watches must be in excellent condition – restoration and damage are rarely acceptable.
- Watches by major Swiss firms – Vacheron, Audemar Piguet, Patek Philippe, IWC – are costly at first, but hold their value.
- Watches by Swatch are worth more in mint, packaged condition.
- Early examples of new technologies are much sought after.

▼ Swatch Irony "ROTOR"

The Swiss company Swatch revolutionized the wristwatch industry with the launch in 1983 of an all-plastic, fully integrated, affordable, and disposable timepiece that one could change to match an outfit. Among the most collectable today are limited editions and those designed by celebrities, such as the automatic "ROTOR" (seen here), which is by the Italian sculptor Arnaldo Pomodoro. Mint boxed condition is a prerequisite for maximum value.

Swiss mechanical, 1997, signed "Arnaldo Pomodoro", £300–450

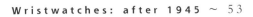

Wristwatches: Rolex

A Rolex remains one of our age's great status symbols. The company was established in Geneva in 1908, and, alongside other Swiss companies such as Patek Philippe and Vacheron & Constantin, established a worldwide reputation that it still enjoys. This is partly due to the company policy of limited production: only a certain number of watches is produced each year, and those are sold only through chosen retailers, with tight control on price; this has ensured a return on investment rarely found with other watches. Rolex's reputation is also due to innovations such as the first waterproof watch – the "Oyster" of 1926 – which had a twinlock system that sealed the winding button against water and dust. Given that every collector would like a Rolex, there is a range of prices to choose from.

Swiss lever, c.1940, signed "Rolex Oyster Perpetual Certified chronometer", **£2,500–4,500**

▼ "Bubble-back" perpetual chronometer
Rolex watches made between 1910 and the 1940s – such as this example – are among the most collectable and sought after, especially those that have the "bubble back". The copper-coloured centre dial has the famous signature and luminous hands and numerals. Even though the 18-carat red-gold "Oyster" case was originally waterproof, it should be checked by a Rolex dealer before risking submersion. The gold screwdown button is marked "Rolex Oyster", and the brown crocodile strap has the Rolex buckle with the Rolex "R" insignia.

▼ Steel and gold "bubble-back" chronometer
Although contemporary with the previous example, with which it shares many features, this perpetual chronometer is less expensive because the "Oyster" case is of stainless steel (rather than gold), with a red-gold bezel. It carries the Rolex signature on the dial and the screwdown button ("Patent Oyster"), and both the strap and gilt buckle are marked. Rolex is punctilious about marking its watches and components, and for maximum value all parts must be of authentic Rolex manufacture.

Swiss lever, c.1940, signed "Rolex Oyster Perpetual Chronometer", **£900–3,000**

Swiss lever, c.1988, signed "Rolex Oyster Perpetual Datejust Superlative Chronometer Officially Certified", **£2,000–5,000**

Swiss lever, c.1990, signed "Rolex", **£3,500–7,000**

▲ Lady's datejust "Oyster"
Datejust Rolex watches show the date only, without the day or month. The design and high-quality movement on this piece are typical of watches produced by the company in the 1990s. Bonus features on this example are the use of sapphire glass, which is very hardwearing and doesn't scratch, the diamond-set dial, and the popular "President" bracelet, which is made up of tight links that conceal the clasp.

▲ Lady's gold "Oyster"
This lady's gold "Oyster" has several desirable features. The signed black dial is set with diamond batons and has an interchangeable white-gold diamond-set bezel, while the case is 18-carat gold, as is the much sought after "President" bracelet. Although a diamond-set dial or bezel is an original Rolex feature, they were also produced by other companies and fitted to original Rolex watches, as were non-original bracelets; both will detract from value.

Swiss lever, c.1989, signed "Rolex", **£2,000–5,000**

▼ Gentleman's day-date "Oyster"
Although both day and date appear on this man's "Oyster", it shares many of the features of the lady's watch above, including a diamond-set dial. Rolex dials are often replaced with non-original dials, which reduce value, as do "President" bracelets with stretched links (it is better to keep the bracelet slightly loose). In general, men's Rolex watches are more sought after than the company's ladies' watches, women having a wider choice of status-symbol jewellery.

Components & accessories

Components and accessories are the ideal starting-point for collectors with limited budgets. There is a vast range to choose from: complete and partial movements, dials, watch cocks, pillars, and remnants of cases, together with accessories such as keys, fobs, watch chains, and chatelaines. Keys and watch cocks are the least expensive, prices starting very low. Broken movements can yield cocks, pillars, and so on, either as collectable items in their own right or as replacement parts for other movements. And every collector of watches dreams of finding a dial by a famous maker, of bringing together a case and a movement that were intended for each other, or of finding a key or a watch that will complete a chatelaine.

▶ **Early English movement**
This late-17thC verge is one of a pair of fine early English movements. Apart from the early date, other collectable features are the unusual tulip pillars with pierced galleries above (pairs of such pillars are sought after for restoration), a typical winged watch cock, and a finely engraved foot and plate for the silver regulator disc. The maker's signature appears on the plate, as happens with most movements. Although the dial and motion work are missing, the early date, unusual pillars, and fine engraving make the movement worth buying in its own right.

English verge, c.1695, signed "Jos Norris Abingdon", **£100–300** for the pair

▼ **Mock pendulum**
The exceptionally finely pierced and engraved cock of this verge movement has had a semi-section cut out to reveal a mock pendulum. This feature – an imitation of the clock pendulum – was very popular during the late 17thC. With early examples such as this it is more important to have the full quota of components, even if they are damaged, than it is for the movement to work. Most will lack their dials and dial plates, which will probably have been used for restoration.

English verge with mock pendulum, c.1695, signed "Jos Foster London", **£250–500**

▼ Movement with dial

The enamel dial on this movement was added later and therefore contributes little to the value, unlike an original dial. The movement, however, is a fine example of both a winged and masked cock, and a pierced and engraved foot, and has desirable Egyptian pillars in good condition. Even though the movement needs cleaning and restoring, it still works intermittently; a good working movement costs 10 to 15 per cent of the full price of a more mundane watch.

▼ Mock pendulum

The interesting feature of this verge movement is that, although it is English, it has a typical continental cock with a mock pendulum. The table cock is screwed down on both sides; it has no foot, no wings, and no masking. The original silver affixes to the straight-sided pillars have been removed — probably for use in restoration. The presence of such an obviously continental design in an English watch is probably the result either of repair work or of a commission for a client living abroad.

English verge, c.1700, signed "John Kirton London", **£100–500**

English verge with mock pendulum, c.1760, signed "Willm Crayton London", **£150–400**

Movements

• Early movements provide less variety of escapement but are rarer and more decorative.
• Movements are found in a vast range of prices.
• Most movements are signed on the back plate.
• Most desirable are good-quality, early watch movements complete with dials and hands.
• Movements by famous makers such as Tompion, Quare and Breguet are sought after; signed examples can be worth around 30 per cent of the total value of a complete watch.

Keys

• Novelty keys are popular but often faked; check for over-bright (or a lack of) gilding and unworn condition.
• Decorative keys should be in good condition (pastes or gems intact; repoussé undamaged; enamel unchipped; and goldwork or gilding in a good clean state).

Cocks

• Watch cocks are available in a vast range of designs and prices.
• Complete examples are essential.
• Late 17thC and early 18thC Dutch examples are rare and desirable.
• Commemorative or historical subjects are very popular.

▼ Keyless fusee

Three features make this movement collectable: the keyless fusee movement itself, signed "Barraud & Lunds" (Barrauds & Lund was founded in 1838, becoming Barraud & Lund in 1846) – a good English maker of the time; the three-piece white enamel dial with power reserve gauge; and an unusual number, "3/3333" (in general, the numbering on English movements is not as important as it is on American watches, where numbered limited-edition movements are much sought after). Although the balance staff is broken, this is a simple and inexpensive repair.

▼ American duplex

The American Waterbury Watch Company (est.1880) was one of the major producers of the inexpensive mass-produced watches that were to become a feature of the 20thC watch industry. Although the duplex escapement that was used on the ingenious and inexpensive Waterbury watches was thought too delicate for long-term reliability, this example of c.1890 is, like many others, still in perfect working order.

▼ Gilt-metal chatelaine

Variety and attractive design make chatelaines a popular niche for collectors. Complete examples – those with their original watches – will be very costly; much more affordable are examples such as this gilt-metal English chatelaine, which is worth 20 to 25 per cent of a complete version. The three sections are decorated with pierced, chased, and engraved figures, with delicate filigree work. If the original watch (or a similar one) is found, the complete piece would be worth at least double the combined value of the individual watch and the chatelaine.

American duplex, c.1890, signed "The Waterbury Watch Co. USA Patented Series N", £10–60

English keyless fusee lever, c.1870, signed "Barraud & Lunds 49 Cornhill London 3/3333", £75–250

English, c.1760, l. 130mm, w. 48mm, £250–750

▼ Framed watch cocks

These watch cocks from the late 18thC and early 19thC are all English, with the exception of the French example in the centre. They give some idea of the ranges of piercing and engraving that make watch cocks decorative and attractive in their own right. The golden age for decorative cocks was 1690 to 1770; much sought after are undamaged early winged cocks, commemorative cocks, those featuring certain subjects such as Nelson, and those numbered and marked by renowned makers such as Graham or Tompion. As a rule, it is less costly to collect and mount individual examples; this also offers the collector an opportunity to become familiar with the changes in design that have taken place across different periods.

English and French watch cocks, c.1720–1850, **£250–500 for the set**

German or Austrian chatelaine, c.1760, **£750–1,500**

▲ Chatelaine with key

The small size and decorative design of this paste-set chatelaine suggest that it was designed for a lady's watch. It is particularly desirable because it is silver set with pastes and has its original key (valuable in its own right). It has paste-set spring clips for other attachments, and is held in place with a gold brooch pin. Probably of German or Austrian origin, it would have come in an attractive fitted case that would be a valuable additional feature.

▼ Keys

As each watch had one, and perhaps a replacement as well, keys can be found in a variety of designs and prices. Shown below are particularly popular novelty designs, such as pistols and shamrocks, as well as more traditional designs. Historical figures such as Napoleon and Nelson are also popular, as, with collectors of jewellery, are decorative gem-set examples.

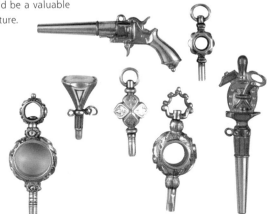

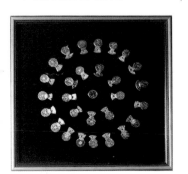

Seven keys, c.1770–1880, **£250–750 for the set**

Glossary

albert Watch chain usually attached to a waistcoat.

arbor A shaft or spindle.

arcaded minute ring Type of arched decoration, commonly used by Dutch makers.

automatic Watch wound by the movements of the wearer.

automaton watch Watch (usually a repeater) with figures or other devices that move.

balance Wheel that controls the going of a watch.

balance spring Spiral spring that regulates timekeeping.

balance staff Arbor to which the inner end of the balance spring is attached.

barrel Barrel-shaped box that houses the mainspring.

bezel Rim that holds the watch glass.

calendar Feature that indicates the day/date/year.

calibre Specification of the type and size of the watch.

cartouche dial Engraved metal dial on which numerals appear in black or blue on white enamel plaques.

centre seconds Seconds hand central to the main dial; often pivoted with the hour and minute hands at the centre.

champlevé enamel Decoration in which an area of metal is hollowed out and filled with enamel.

chapter ring Ring marked with hours, minutes, or half and quarter-hours.

chasing Method of decoration using hammers and punches to push metal into a relief pattern.

chronograph Watch with a centre seconds hand that functions as a stop watch.

chronometer Watch with a detent escapement; also the Swiss term for a very accurate movement.

cloisonné Decoration in which the enamel is fired in *cloisons* (or compartments) outlined in flat metal wire.

cock Plate, one end of which supports the balance staff, the other of which is fixed to the movement plate.

compensation balance Balance that compensates for changes in temperature.

consular case Case that resembles a pair case with a high rounded glass. Popular in France, and introduced during, and supposedly named after, the period when Napoleon was Consul.

crab-tooth duplex Duplex escapement on which the teeth on the locking wheel resemble crabs' claws. Used mainly on watch intended for export to China.

cuvette Inner hinged and sprung cover used to protect the movement.

cylinder Escapement that is laid out horizontally, allowing for slimmer watches.

date aperture Small opening on the dial through which the date is displayed.

detent Component used on a chronometer primarily to minimize the escape wheel's inteference with the balance.

dial plate Plate to which the dial is fixed.

digital dial Dial without hands on which hours and minutes are instead shown by numerals.

duplex Escapement with two sets of teeth – one for locking, one for giving impulse.

ébauche Rough or partly finished movements.

endstone Jewel set in a ring in the cock against which a pivot end bears.

en-grisaille painted decoration using a mainly black and grey palette and resembling a print.

engine turning Decorative, textured patterns created by turning metal on an machine-driven lathe.

escapement Part of the movement that controls the driving power and gives impulse to the balance.

escape wheel Last wheel in the train that gives impulse to the balance.

flyback hand Hand that "flies" back to zero or to join another hand.

foot Part of the cock that is fixed to the plate.

form watch Watch with case that resembles another object.

fusee Conical spool that evens out the uneven pull of a mainspring as it unwinds.

gilt (metal) Silver or other metal to which a thin layer of gold has been applied.

going barrel Barrel, with a wheel on the outer edge, containing the mainspring.

hairspring Common name for the balance spring.

half-hunter case Case with a central aperture in the front lid to show the dial and hands.

helical hairspring Balance spring formed into a helix, often used with chronometer or detent escapements.

hunter case (or full-hunter case) Watch case with a solid cover to the dial.

jacquemart (or jack) Figure or automaton that strikes the bell on repeater watches.

jewelled Movement bearings of precious or semi-precious stone used to reduce friction.

lever Escapement in which the impulse is transmitted by a lever.

lugs part of wristwatch to which strap is attached.

mainspring Spring that provides the driving power for the watch.

maintaining power Device for driving a watch movement that would otherwise stop when it was being wound.

micrometer regulator Regulator on the hairspring for fine adjustment.

mock pendulum Small disc on one arm of the balance that moves and imitates a clock pendulum.

motion work The wheels and pinions beneath the dial that drive the hands.

oignon Large and bulbous watch made in France in the late 17thC and early 18thC.

open-face case Case without a front cover.

pair case Watch with two cases: an inner case to house the movement and an outer protective case, sometimes decorative.

pallet Part or parts of the escapement on which the escape wheel acts.

perpetual calendar Calendar watch that allows for short months and leap years without manual adjustment.

pinion The driven gear, with teeth known as "leaves".

piqué (pin work) Gold, silver, or brass pins used, often in a decorative pattern, to secure a covering to an outer pair case.

power reserve indicator Subsidiary dial that shows the state of the winding.

regulator disc Disc used to adjust the hairspring to regulate the watch.

repeater Movement that chimes the time on demand.

repoussé Decoration using hammers and punches to push metal into a relief pattern; more precisely the secondary process of chasing metal.

rolled gold Heavy gold plate applied to another metal.

screwback watch Watch in which the back is screwed down rather than hinged.

self-winding (or perpetual) watch Watch wound by the movements of the wearer.

subsidiary dial Small extra dial, often showing seconds, set within the main dial.

table (cock) The part of the cock that covers the balance and provides the bearing for the balance staff.

table roller lever Lever escapement with the impulse pin mounted on a flat disc.

train Series of wheels and pinions geared to one another that transmits power.

verge Earliest escapement, with an escape wheel that resembles a crown with triangular teeth.

watch paper Small circular pieces of paper or fabric placed in the back of the outer pair case to protect the inner case, eliminate slack between the cases, and advertise the watchmaker.

Where to buy

Novice collectors are advised to buy from reputable dealers (members of LAPADA and BADA), established auction houses, and other outlets where they will be given a written receipt, possibly with a condition report, and will be able to return a watch that does not match the description under which it was sold.

COLLECTOR'S GROUPS

Collectors' groups meet and arrange selling shows throughout the country. Details can be found in local directories and in the periodicals *Antiquarian Horology* and *British Horological Journal*.

AUCTION HOUSES

Bonhams (Chelsea)
65–9 Lots Road
London SW10 0RN

Christie's
8 King Street
St James's
London SW1Y 6QT

Phillips
101 New Bond Street
London W1Y 0AS

Sotheby's
34–35 New Bond Street
London W1A 2AA

DEALERS

London
A.S. Antiques
Unit 38
The Bond Street
Antique Centre
124 New Bond Street
London W1Y 9AE
Tel: 0171 629 3008

Anthony Green Antiques
Unit 39
The Bond Street
Antique Centre
124 New Bond Street
London W1Y 9AE
Tel: 0171 409 2854

Charles Frodsham & Co Ltd
32 Bury Street
London SW1Y 6AU.
Tel: 0171 839 1234

Graus Antiques
Bond Street Silver Galleries
111–12 New
Bond Street
London W1Y 0BQ
Tel: 0171 629 6680

Nonesuch Antiques
Unit 4
The Bond Street
Antique Centre
124 New Bond Street
London W1Y 9AE
Tel: 0171 629 6783

Somlo Antiques
7 Piccadilly Arcade
London SW1
Tel: 0171 499 6526

Johnny Wachsmann
Pieces of Time
1–7 Davies Mews
Unit 17–19
London W1Y 2LP
Tel: 0171 629 2422
(24-hr)/629 3272
Fax: 0171 409 1625
Internet: http://www.antique-watch.com
E-mail: info@antique-watch.com

Outside London
Boodles & Dunthorne
52 Eastgate Street
Chester
Cheshire CH1 1ES
Tel: 01244 326666

Boodles & Dunthorne
Boodles House
Lord Street
Liverpool L2 9SQ
Tel: 0151 227 2525

What to read

GENERAL

Britten, F.J. *Old Clocks and Watches and their Makers* (London, 1982)

Bruton, E. *The History of Clocks and Watches* (London, 1979)

Jagger, C. *The World's Greatest Clocks and Watches* (London, 1977)

WATCHES

Clutton, C. and Daniels, G. *Watches: A Complete History of the Technical and Decorative Development of the Watch* (London, 1979)

Cuss, T.P. *The Camerer Cuss Book of Antique Watches* (Woodbridge, 1976)

Cutmore, M. *The Watch Collector's Handbook* (Newton Abbot, 1976)

Cutmore, M. *The Pocket Watch Handbook* (Newton Abbot, 1985)

Ehrhardt, R. and Meggers, B. *American Watches: Beginning to End 1830–1980: Identification and Price Guide* (Florida, 1986)

Harrold, M.C. *American Watchmaking* (Columbia, PA, 1984)

Hoke, D. *American Pocket Watches* (Rockford, 1991)

Jagger, C. *The Artistry of the English Watch* (Newton Abbot, 1988)

Kemp, R. *The Englishman's Watch* (Altrincham, 1979)

Shenton, A. *Pocket Watches: 19th & 20th Century* (Woodbridge, 1995)

MAKERS

Daniels, G. *The Art of Breguet* (London, 1975)

Loomes, B. *Watchmakers & Clockmakers of the World* (London, 1976)

SPECIALIST BOOKSHOPS

Rita Shenton Horological Books
142 Percy Road, Twickenham, TW2 6JG. Tel: 0181 894 6888.

G.K. Hadfield
Rock Farm, Chilcote, Swadlincote, Derbyshire, DE12 8DQ. Tel: 01827 373466

Index & acknowledgments

Picture Acknowledgments
Bulgari **52r**; Octopus Publishing Group Ltd. **43bl**, **51bl**, Octopus Publishing Group Ltd./Steve Tanner **front
cover**, **2**, **34l**, **35tl**, **35tr**, **35b**, **36t**, **36b**, **37l**, **37tr**, **37br**, **38l**, **38r**, **39t**, **39c**, **39b**, **40l**, **40c**, **40r**, **41l**,
41r, **42l**, **42r**, **43t**, **43br**, **44l**, **44r**, **45l**, **45c**, **45r**, **46l**, **46r**, **47t**, **47b**, **48t**, **48b**, **49t**, **49bl**, **49br**, **50l**,
50r, **51t**, **51br**, **52l**, **53t**, **53b**, **54l**, **55tr**, **55tl**, **55b**, **56t**, **56b**, **57l**, **57t**, **58l**, **58c**, **58r**, **59t**, **59bl**, **59br**;
Swatch/Stefan Minder **53 br**; Johnny Wachsmann/Alan Grant **1**, **5**, **6t**, **6 b**, **7**, **8l**, **8tr**, **8br**, **14l**, **14r**, **15t**,
15c, **15b**, **16t**, **16b**, **17l**, **17r**, **18l**, **18c**, **18r**, **19tl**, **19tr**, **19b**, **20l**, **20r**, **21t**, **21bl**, **21br**, **22l**, **22r**, **23tl**,
23tr, **23b**, **24t**, **24b**, **25l**, **25c**, **25r**, **26l**, **26r**, **27c**, **27l**, **27r**, **28t**, **28b**, **29l**, **29r**, **30l**, **30c**, **30r**, **31tl**,
31tr, **31b**, **32l**, **32r**, **33l**, **33r**, **34r**.